DANCING PRIEST

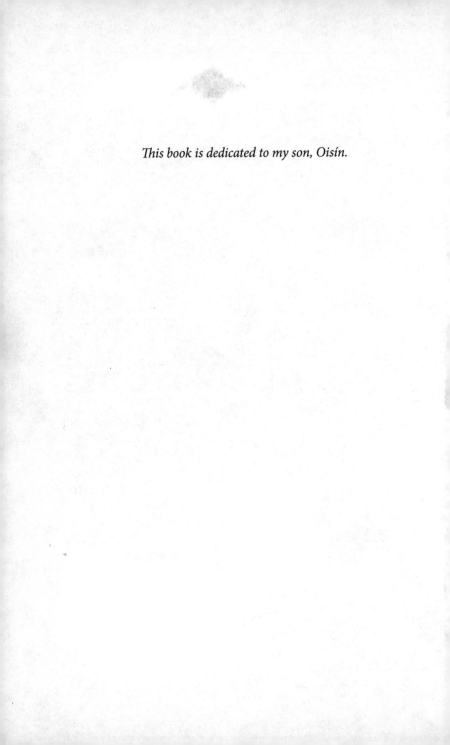

This book is dedicated to my son, Oisín.

DANCING PRIEST

THE FATHER NEIL HORAN STORY

AIDAN O'CONNOR

LONDUBH BOOKS

First published by Londubh Books 2010

Londubh Books, 18 Casimir Avenue, Harold's Cross, Dublin 6w

1 3 5 4 2

Cover by bluett; cover images © Press Association

Origination by Londubh Books

Printed in Ireland by ColourBooks, Baldoyle Industrial Estate, Dublin 13

ISBN: 978-1907535-07-9

CONTENTS

ACKNOWLEDGEMENTS

This book would not have been possible without the help of many people who gave generously of their time and effort. Special thanks to Neil Horan for his honesty and cooperation. I am most grateful to Rob Armstrong and his wife Barbara who offered their support and encouragement from the very outset. The people interviewed for this book include Derek Hilsden, Delia McManus, Teresa Lennon, Kathy Mullin, Sophie Hicks, Richard Kozieros, Kathy Denning, Dan Horan and members of the UK Police and the Catholic Church (Ireland and UK).

Of great value was reference material provided by many media organisations including the *Daily Telegraph*, the *Sunday Telegraph*, the *South London Press*, the *Southwark News*, the *Irish World*, the *Irish Post*, the *Portsmouth News*, the *Catholic Herald*, the *Dartford Times*, the *Observer*, the *Kentish Times*, the *Gravesend and Dartford Extra*, the *Independent* (London), the *Sun*, the *Mirror*, Press Association, Reuters, *The Irish Times*, the *Irish Independent*, the *Examiner*, the *Star*, the *Irish Daily Mail*, the *Sunday World*, the *Sunday Tribune*, the *Kerryman*, *Kerry's Eye*, the *Kingdom*, BBC, ITV and SKY.

I am also grateful to Jo O'Donoghue and everyone associated with Londubh Books, including designer Syd Bluett and publicist Hugh O'Donoghue, for having the courage and belief to publish this book, and to friends and family members and many current and former journalist colleagues for their advice and support.

PROLOGUE

Father Neil Horan grew nervous as he approached the British Airways check-in desk at London's Gatwick Airport. It was Saturday afternoon, 28 August 2004.

The young staff member opened the passport, glanced at Horan, then cordially asked the priest if he was travelling to Athens for the Olympic Games.

'No I'm not,' came the reply. 'I've a great interest in Athens. It's a very historic and interesting city. I'll be doing a bit of sightseeing.'

Twenty-four hours later, the world would witness one of the most bizarre moments in sporting history. The Kerry-born priest would fling off his full-length white coat to display Biblical placards pinned to a dancing costume comprising an orange kilt, green socks and green underpants. Diving under a tape barrier, Horan would run on to the Olympic marathon course and bundle race leader Vanderlei de Lima to the ground, smashing the Brazilian's hopes of winning gold.

Horan never really knew how his publicity stunt in Athens would unfold. He claims it was never his intention to touch or harm de Lima. But what he was clear about was his intention to hijack one of the world's greatest sporting events to gain publicity for his lifelong message: that the second coming of Jesus Christ is near.

It was the second time the priest had come to world attention.

A year before, he had run on to the race track at the Silverstone Grand Prix circuit.

Travelling at up to 200kmph, Formula One racing cars swerved to avoid the priest. Miraculously, nobody was injured in the incident.

Horan was crowned a nutter. For months afterwards he was subjected to ridicule by the press. He became the priest who was at war with the Catholic Church over his interpretations of the Bible and whose antics were making him a marked man among police authorities all over the world.

Few knew much about the man behind the scandals. Throughout his life, even family members struggled to comprehend his actions and the lengths to which Neil Horan was willing to go to promote his message: 'Read the Bible'.

Horan has devoted his adult life to studying scripture. He has successfully won the attention of world media, police authorities, the Vatican and two successive Popes.

But who could really lie behind the outrageous publicity stunts? What beliefs could push an intelligent, articulate priest to the point where he was sacked by the Vatican, remanded in prison and kept under observation by international police?

How could a shy, soft-spoken Catholic priest from rural Ireland bring shame on himself and all those around him?

And if this man is mad, how is it that doctors not alone differed, but totally disagreed on his mental health?

1

THE LONER CHILD

It was hopeless. No matter how hard he tried, young Neil Horan just couldn't catch the small ball any time it was thrown to him. 'Butterhands!' the others called out. The comments hurt. It was easier to hide away.

By the end of his first year's education in primary school, six-year-old Horan's most striking personality traits were becoming abundantly clear. The few daily hours outside his home and away from the familiarity of the family farm were difficult. Sixty years on, the memories of those early years still hurt.

'I was painfully shy. I found mixing most difficult and even as a young boy I was very tense. I tended to see only the serious side of life, and while my brother Pat laughed and joked on his way to school, I worried about what the day might hold.'

School was never like home. The seventy acres of damp and rushy farmland around Knockeenahone in Scartaglen was safe and familiar. It was enough to provide the Horan family with a comfortable living. Neil's father, Humphrey, known as 'Free', worked the farm with his wife Nellie while the couple reared fourteen children, eight boys and six girls. Neil, born in 1947, was the second eldest.

Horan's early childhood was typical of rural Kerry in the 1950s. Warm summers were laced with long and lazy days spent cutting turf in Daly's bog in Tooreengariffe Glen. The Horans were a close family and rural life for a child around Scartaglen was carefree and fun. 'Like most young boys, I loved the feel of the fine day, the feel of the sun beating down as we made our way to the bog or made wynds of hay in the fields. I can remember too the sense of adventure when a few of us would climb the hill near Tooreen and look over the Brown Flesk river winding its way through the neighbouring lands.'

As the eldest son, Horan's future could have very well rested in farming the Sliabh Luachra land where he was born and reared. He was good around the farm, obliging and interested. However, by the time he had finished primary education, young Horan had chosen religious life and religious life had been chosen for him.

Farming, GAA, traditional music and religion dominated most of the conversations in homes around Scartaglen. Every evening, after the Horans finished work on the farm, they gathered in the kitchen and went on bended knee to recite the Rosary. Moreover, the extended Horan family was steeped in religious life. Neil's uncle, Father John, and his aunt, Sister Anthony, were both significant influences throughout Horan's early life.

As a child, Horan was an average pupil. He struggled with maths and Irish but quickly established a keen interest in history. However, it was religion, taught then in primary school as Catechism, that truly captured the child's imagination.

The rehearsed answers to religious questions in school appeared to fascinate him the most. Questions like, 'Why did God make me?' met with a regurgitated answer: 'To know, love and serve Him in this life and to be happy with Him forever in the next.'

But for young Horan, the answers were more than stock replies. He found the Catechism 'majestic and clear'. Not alone was it simple, 'it all had lofty sentiments about it as well'.

From a very early age, Neil Horan felt he could deal with his crippling shyness and the struggle at school by thoughts of following in his Uncle John's footsteps and embracing religious life. The cruel and lonely world created by shyness and a sense of difference was temporary. Deep down he believed that one day, the Roman collar would change all that.

One late summer's evening while on holiday in his grandmother's house, Neil and his brother Pat got ready for bed. True to form, Hannah O'Sullivan entered the bedroom to say goodnight to her grandchildren. It is a moment Neil clearly remembers and one that flagged the direction of his entire future.

'My grandmother turned to Pat and asked him, "And what will you be, Pat, when you are big?"

'"A farmer," Pat replied.

'"And what about you Neilie?"

'"I think I'd like to be a priest," I said.

'My grandmother paused and looked at me. "You'll be a little priesteen, Neilie, you'll wear the Roman collar." I must have been no more than eight.' His grandmother's words on that night would remain with Horan for years to come, ultimately proving poignant and ironic.

Throughout his early years, Horan's fascination with religious life was influenced largely by his uncle John. Ordained in 1942, Father John returned home from Leeds to Scartaglen twice every year. The stories he told and his way of life appealed to Neil, so much so that he decided it was a life he wanted for himself.

He had always wanted to be like his uncle. Fascinated by his articulate speech and knowledge of world affairs, he looked up to him and was in no doubt that there was something different about his uncle when compared to all other men he knew.

For the young boy, Uncle John seemed more educated, his conversation 'a bit higher than the common farmers around Knockeenahone'. Father John had something the others hadn't got. Whatever that was, Neil wanted it too.

About one-third of Horan's class moved from primary school in Knockeenahone to a private secondary school in Castleisland.

For the first time, the young teenager was forced to mix with boys born in an urban setting. They were different from the country boys from nearby Scartaglen; not necessarily brighter at school, but far more cunning and streetwise.

For that first year in Castleisland, Horan dodged and ducked again. His fear of getting hurt or injured made him the exception when it came to football. His shyness prevented him from asking questions in class and no tears were shed when Father John suggested he move to school in Mount Melleray in County Waterford to continue his schooling. It was a Cistercian monastery Father John had attended. It also had a philosophy department that clerical students attended.

Nellie cried as she and Free drove away from Melleray in their blue Prefect car, having dropped Neil off there for the first time. The fourteen-year-old's heart sank as he waved goodbye. He would now be away from home for the first time. It was early September 1961 and the fourteen weeks to Christmas seemed an eternity.

Within weeks of his arrival at Melleray, the large boarding dormitories and homesickness became too much for Horan. After school, he would walk alone for miles, thinking of the hill in Tooreen and the long lazy evenings spent in Daly's bog.

'I nearly died of heartbreak at the foot of the Knockmealdown

Mountains. It was pure downright homesickness every day I was there.

'After school I'd watch farmers around working with barley and oats. It would bring my thoughts back to my father and my Uncle Mike working the farm at home.

'I'd walk for hours in the evenings alone, not one student speaking to me nor I speaking to them. That's the way it was. I was painfully shy and totally out of my depth.

'The older lads would point me out and say, "That man looks lonesome." I don't know how I stuck it there. If the stones around Melleray could talk they'd tell a story because I died every day I spent there.'

At the end of the summer break after his first year in Melleray, Horan remained unusually quiet in himself as his father drove the long and dreaded journey back to County Waterford. A school report had been sent home, one that Neil knew would not impress his parents and one he hoped would never be raised in conversation. But it was. Free turned to Neil in the car and remarked that he thought his son would have done better in his first year. The young lad burst into tears. 'I did my best, Dada', came the reply.

Horan just about passed his Intermediate Certificate exam but had enough of Melleray and life away from home. By now, neighbours and relations around Scartaglen spoke openly of how the young student would become a priest one day.

While his longing for the priesthood remained solid, school in Melleray was a hurdle too high. It simply could no longer be part of the plan.

On a summer's morning while on holidays at home, the sixteen-year-old climbed high in the loft of the barn outside. Unable to face his parents with what he had to say, he waited until Free and Nellie were busy milking the cows. With pen and paper in hand, the troubled teenager began to write a letter to his parents.

> Dear Mama and Dada, I am writing to you to tell you I don't want to go back to Melleray. It's too sad. The dormitories, the football, nobody speaking to me in the refectory, it's all too much…

The lengthy letter told his parents how the others jeered and chanted, 'Horan, Horan, Horan,' when he was called to perform at the Christmas concert the previous year.

He told them of the sneering comments made by classmates as he stood alone; how on the football field he just ran in the opposite direction each time the ball came towards him. He described the long walks alone, the plans to run away, how he felt like a loner and an island. Horan left the letter on his parents' bed. For weeks, they said nothing to him and he said nothing to them.

At the beginning of the next school year in September, Neil suggested he move closer to home and continue his schooling somewhere else. His parents agreed. He attended the Christian Brothers School in Tralee and passed his exams with relative ease. But he failed Latin, a subject crucial for entry to a seminary if he was to study for the priesthood.

Father John suggested he repeat his Leaving Certificate in St Brendan's College in Killarney, the diocesan college. The college was near home but Neil found lodgings in the town and was a day-pupil among the boarders. He passed all subjects with ease, including Latin, and even got honours in some. The path to priesthood was back on track.

To this day, Horan still can't explain what it was about cities and bright lights that attracted him.

About one third of his classmates from St Brendan's went on to study for the priesthood, mainly in Maynooth, and his decision to choose Clonliffe College in Dublin for his studies was unusual. It was a college that trained clerical students solely for the Dublin diocese. The young man who had developed a keen sense of self-awareness about his own shyness and homesickness was inexplicably drawn to the bustle of the capital city.

Within months, Horan was questioning the wisdom of his decision to choose the bright city lights and move to Clonliffe. He found life in Dublin desperately difficult. His relationships with fellow-students were pitiful, even non-existent. Very soon the gulf that existed between the Dublin students and the country boy from Kerry was proving too much. Horan knew he just wasn't fitting in.

Again, he struggled on the sporting field, often going to catch the ball over his head when playing soccer. Even then, he couldn't seem to make the catch.

It was all because of the fear, he claimed. But a new and strange symptom also began to rear its head for the first time.

Horan began to find himself making more and more trips to the bathroom to wash his hands, to the point where the practice became obsessive. His hands appeared to sweat and feel sticky, especially when he became nervous or felt under pressure.

Before anybody else found out, he planned his own trip to see a doctor. He knew full well something was wrong within. The sticky and sweaty hands were clearly linked to his nervous disposition. The first doctor he visited referred him to Father Joe Carroll, the college president. From there, Horan was sent to a psychiatrist for further examination.

His first trip to Doctor Des McGrath in Fitzgibbon Square in Dublin in the New Year of 1967 began a long and controversial relationship with the psychiatric profession. Over five visits in two months, Horan explained his difficulties to Dr McGrath. The crippling shyness, the compulsion to constantly wash his sticky and sweaty hands and the never-ending struggle to relate to others all led Dr McGrath to arrive at a conclusion: Horan was suffering from a compulsive nervous disorder.

During his final visit, Dr McGrath sat the student down for a candid talk. He outlined the realities of his condition and explained that it would hinder his life as a practising priest. What he was telling Horan was not in the plan.

'I recall him telling me how I wasn't suitable for the priesthood. I just wouldn't be able to deal with large congregations and public life would prove too much for me.

'But I insisted I was cut out for this life. It was shocking to me then that he was suggesting, without directly saying it but by implication, that the priesthood was not for me.

'I thought to myself there and then that this guy was going to ruin everything. He was going to stop me becoming a priest.'

Soon after, college president Father Joe Carroll summoned Horan to his office. He sat him down and relayed to him the conclusions of his own discussions with Dr McGrath. He told Horan that he might have gifts in other areas and that all other career doors were not closed to him. But the priesthood was.

Horan left that meeting with a clear and unambiguous understanding of what was happening. He was being kicked out of college.

Father Carroll agreed to help ease the pain of what had happened by sparing Horan the dreaded prospect of having to tell his family the news.

On a sleety day in spring 1967, a letter from the college president arrived at the Horan home in Scartaglen. Free sat in the armchair in the kitchen corner and read the letter to himself before lifting his head and turning to Neil and others gathered round. "'Tis bad news,' he said. 'After all the trouble we went to. 'Tis all over now.'

News of what had happened spread around Scartaglen like a gorse fire in May. Young Horan was not returning to college and was no longer going to be a priest. In their small rural community, the news came as a massive blow to the extended Horan family. It was unthinkable disappointment and shame.

For weeks it was almost like a death: the incident cast a shadow over the extended family. Neil Horan would probably have inherited the farm had he not chosen the priesthood.

His entire family, including his grandmother, had spoken about the eldest son becoming a priest for the previous ten years. All the relatives knew, with many sparing a thought for Aunt Bridie who had paid for Horan's education.

For Horan, the episode was a sorry affair. He felt he had let himself down. And he believed his father thought, as he put it, that 'their son was a failure and hadn't delivered what they hoped'. Horan decided to move on. For a while, at least, he would ditch the priesthood plans and take time to think it all over. He left Scartaglen for Dublin to work, away from family and neighbours and the constant queries about his future in the Catholic Church.

Without any great difficulty, he secured a job in a farm food factory on the Naas Road outside Dublin. The work was straightforward, stacking cattle feed bags and unloading foodstuffs from lorries.

But within months Horan came to the conclusion that he still wanted religious life. Dublin proved the ideal break he needed to plan his return to the priesthood, giving him the discipline of hard work and time to clear his mind.

Horan believed he could return to Melleray to resume his studies and finish his second year of philosophy. He could then move on somewhere else, anywhere, to finish his studies for the priesthood. Things appeared to be looking up. Until one evening in March 1968 when James Leydon arrived to the front office of Horan's workplace. It was close on 5.30pm and Neil was about to leave. Leydon shared accommodation with Horan, and while they were good friends, his unannounced appearance was unusual in the extreme.

Leydon was pale-faced. He looked at his room-mate and relayed the message. Hannah, Neil's younger sister, had died suddenly at home but Leydon could provide no details of what had happened. Horan immediately made his way to the station. Before boarding the last train to Kerry, he rang the postmaster in Scartaglen to find out more. His sixteen-year-old sister had died from a brain haemorrhage and funeral arrangements had already been made. For then, that was all he knew.

Hannah had been waked in the house that day and her remains taken to the local church. But Neil's late arrival from Dublin meant he did not have the chance to say his final farewell. That night, an exception was made and the coffin was re-opened in the church. Near the altar in Scartaglen church, Horan saw his sister for the last time and said goodbye.

Hannah was an exceptional young girl. She had completed her Intermediate exams the year before and was a highly intelligent student. The local newspaper, *The Kerryman*, had remarked on Hannah's academic achievements, describing her as a 'brilliant pupil'.

Hannah's sudden illness took everybody by surprise. She was a healthy, outgoing girl who had apparently fallen mildly ill the previous day and was sent home from school to recover. But by the time her local doctor examined her, Hannah had become gravely ill. By the time an ambulance arrived, she was dead.

Neil and Hannah had grown particularly close. The previous year, they had cycled to and from Killarney where they worked during the summer holidays.

Even as a young teenager, Hannah showed a maturity way beyond her tender years. She regularly conversed about life, politics and issues that would have been of little interest to other girls her age. To Neil, she was the one who stood out in the family. 'No question, Hannah was different from every other member of the family. She had a sweet innocence, yet stood out by her ability to have serious discussions.'

The young girl's death created a dark cloud over the close-knit community around Scartaglen. At the funeral, schoolfriends wept as they stood in a guard of honour for their classmate. There were more questions than answers. How could an intelligent, happy and perfectly healthy girl suddenly fall ill and die? And why should it happen to a family that was God-fearing, God-loving and law-abiding?

The Horan family struggled to deal with Hannah's death. Nellie took it hardest of all, often drifting for long periods into deep thought, perplexed and broken-hearted.

For Horan, it was a stark reminder of life's cruel ways. It heightened his natural melancholy and forced him to conclude: 'The sooner we're out of this world the better, for it's no more than a vale of tears'.

But instead of shaking his religious beliefs, Hannah's death appeared to strengthen them. Hannah had asked him the previous Christmas about what the future had in store and if he was still going to be a priest.

'I recall what she asked and how I told her I hoped one day to be a priest, despite all that had happened. Her death made me more determined to go on. I am somebody who is made more determined by obstacles and setbacks and her passing pushed me on towards college life again.'

Despite their awareness of his history and his experiences at Clonliffe, the authorities at Mount Melleray willingly accepted Horan back for one year to finish his philosophy studies. That year saw a marked change in the young man's outlook and behaviour. Even though his heart was heavy as a result of Hannah's death, he gradually began to mix better with other students and applied himself well to his studies. He had got a second chance and he was determined to take it.

Before the Easter break, hundreds gathered in Melleray's main hall for the annual college concert. They watched in amazement as the young Kerry clerical student took to the stage. For those who knew him, it was a transformation. The young man once crippled by shyness and who shrank from the limelight was dancing a jig on stage.

The weekly dancing lessons he took from master dancer and renowned teacher Rory O'Connor while working in Dublin the previous year were paying off. Horan came from a proud tradition. His homeland of Scartaglen was anchored in the heart of Sliabh Luachra, a geographically undefined region on the Cork-Kerry border, soaked in traditional music, song and dance.

The young student could never sing or play but he was definitely willing to dance. He was proudly flying the Sliabh Luachra flag and now his efforts on stage drew rapturous applause. Horan stole the show and silenced the naysayers. He was no longer an onlooker and outsider. Horan was Melleray's dancing priest.

His next four years, the remainder of his studies for the priesthood, passed without a hitch at St Peter's College in Wexford. The homesickness had gone and Horan's wandering days appeared to be over. By the time he finished at St Peter's, the sticky hands, the overwhelming shyness and the reluctance to settle were faint memories of the past. They now seemed nothing more than minor setbacks that had been successfully overcome.

On 17 June 1973, hundreds of people packed St Mary's Cathedral in Killarney. The sun shone that summer day as Horan knelt before the altar to be ordained. Over him stood the Bishop of Kerry, Eamon Casey, a high-profile figure in the Catholic Church. At that very time – but kept secret from the congregation and the world – Casey was involved in a fully-fledged relationship with American divorcée Annie Murphy. The following year, Casey's secret lover gave birth to his son. The scandal didn't break until 1992 and then it rocked the Catholic Church in Ireland to its foundations.

The night before they were to be ordained, Horan and two other clerics stayed in the bishop's palace in Killarney, rehearsing proceedings for the following day.

Bishop Eamon Casey made the biggest day of Horan's life seem like a stroll in Daly's bog. The bishop's laid-back approach calmed nerves and his sense of humour and warmth removed any last-minute doubts about religious life in the Catholic Church. 'He was as good as any bishop I've seen for ceremonies. He was a people's bishop, a gregarious man with a personal touch. He was dynamic and, of course, he was a major personality at the time, having been on television and radio on many occasions.'

The following night, neighbours, relatives and friends packed

Horan's local church in Scartaglen for his first Mass.

The once-troubled teenager had made it, all the way to the pulpit. All the issues concerning his dismissal from Clonliffe College and the peculiarities of his personality throughout his teenage years had been forgotten and absolved. For the Horan family, things had come full circle. It was a moment most families of the time dreamt of and many prayed for.

As the sound of music and set-dancing poured from the Horan farmhouse that night, Hannah O'Sullivan walked to the front door for some fresh air. On her way back in, she met her newly-ordained grandson, the young man she had told almost twenty years earlier that one day he would wear the Roman collar.

She was right. Beaming with pride, Hannah grasped Neil's hand and congratulated him. 'You're a priesteen now, Neilie, at last,' she said. 'Take good care of it.'

2

A NEW FAMILY

Light snow fell from early morning in Bexley, London. Horan glanced out the window of the presbytery and wondered whether it was safe to go for his regular Sunday cycle. It was 10 February 1974. The newly-ordained priest had followed in his Uncle John's footsteps to the UK and was settling well into his first post as a Catholic curate.

The thin blanket of snow forced Horan to cycle more slowly and cautiously. As he passed a lamp-post in nearby Dartford, a poster caught his eye and he pulled the brakes.

He dismounted from his bike and walked back a few steps to take a closer look. The poster read: 'Signs of the end of this present age. Lecture here at 6.30pm.'

The poster intrigued the young priest. With little else on the parish schedule, later that evening Horan returned in civilian clothes to the Masonic Hall in Dartford to satisfy his curiosity.

Inside, a young Derek Hilsden sat among the twenty-five to thirty people gathered to hear the lecture. He was chatting to others around him when he was distracted by a slight young man wearing thick-rimmed glasses coming through the front door. Hilsden watched as Horan shyly made his way in and took a seat at the back of the hall.

Horan listened for the next hour as Rai Barnett, the group's elder, delivered a lecture on Bible teaching. Barnett spoke of the return of the Jews to the land of Israel; the return of Jesus Christ to earth as king and ruler of the world and how world events were clearly showing that the second appearance of Christ and the end of the world were nigh.

The lecture baffled the young priest. Despite years of religious study, he'd never before heard such a take on the Bible and its contents. During his training in college, he had studied the Bible from a historical perspective. But prophecy or interpretation of the Scriptures never featured. Naturally sceptical, Horan wondered if what Barnett preached was true.

'I thought they were Protestants. I remember telling myself to be careful about what I was dealing with. I had no understanding of Biblical prophecy up to then. I had studied certain facts about the Bible, but knew nothing about interpreting what it said.'

After the lecture, Hilsden and his father-in-law Barnett approached the newcomer and explained to him about the group. They introduced themselves as members of the Apostolic Fellowship of Christ, a small group derived from the Christadelphians that met every Sunday to study and discuss the Bible.

Fearful of what he had got himself into, Horan introduced himself as Con Ryan, an Irish navvy working in nearby Bexley.

Hilsden and Barnett explained the basics of their foundation and beliefs. As a group of 'brothers' and 'sisters', they accepted and professed the doctrines and precepts of Christ as taught in the Scriptures.

They explained that world events heralded the imminent return of Christ to earth as ruler of the world.

The group's study of Biblical prophecy largely had to do with the destiny of nations and the role many of the world's countries would play at Armageddon and during Christ's reign after the second coming. Hilsden later explained in his book *The Last Days*, published in March 2008, that the Bible is a small library of books written over many centuries by men of widely differing backgrounds in many contrasting situations, but always Jews. When it comes to the scope of the prophecies, some were fulfilled within a generation. Others took centuries to be realised and many have not yet been fulfilled.

Hilsden explained that the subject matter of some of the prophecies was more than 2500 years remote from the minds of the individual who received them. Because of this, modern nations are referred to either by the names of the ancient territories, by the names of the peoples whose descendants con-stitute these nations, or by certain marked characteristics clearly identifiable by those living in an era contemporary with the fulfillment of the prophecy.

But the failure to take the language of prophecy as figurative has led to enormous problems, according to Hilsden. The language of prophecy is taken from an analogy between the natural world and the political world. National identities, governments and institutions are often represented by symbols. The literal 'heavens', for example, are taken as the representative of the ruling powers and the 'earth' as those who are ruled over.

The 'sun' represents government vested in the king or emperor, while the 'moon' represents ecclesiastical authorities.

The 'stars' stand for subordinate princes, ministers and generals, while the 'sea' and the 'rivers' are often used figuratively for people of different nations.

A stormy sea, therefore, is representative of nations in conflict; an overflowing river is representative of a conquering army. Mountains stand for great empires and hills for lesser powers, whereas valleys represent oppressed people.

Predatory animals, too, are often used to symbolise aggressive nations, just as the lion is still used to represent Britain, the bear to represent Russia and the frog or cock to represent France.

According to Hilsden, the conciseness of such figurative language helps to reduce the history of a particular nation, people or event to its essential features.

But even the group which Horan first encountered on that February Sunday in 1974 warned of the tendency for some to interpret prophecy by current events in the belief that current-day events are vastly more significant than those of preceding generations.

According to Hilsden, such misguided endeavours not only have the effect of making their advocates seem somewhat foolish when a year or two later their forecast appears false, they distort the meaning of scripture and bring the whole subject of Bible prophecy into disrepute in the public mind.

The Fellowship's core set of beliefs was something Horan had never before encountered. The marked differences to Catholic teaching also began to emerge, not least the belief that the 'Kingdom' would come to earth as opposed to those who die going to the Kingdom.

Hilsden explains that the Fellowship held no animosity towards Catholics but did feel sorry for them. They believe in one God and do not accept the Trinity. For them, Jesus is the son of God, but not God the son.

They believe that the second appearance of Christ will be sparked by an invasion of Israel, spearheaded by Russia, accompanied by a confederacy of France, Germany, Libya, Ethiopia and Iran. It will appear that Israel is facing annihilation But it is then that Jesus will return, giving eternal life to those who are worthy and saving Israel from destruction.

Those who do not believe will die but will not go to hell. As Hilsden explains: 'A loving God never intended to have an eternal barbecue.'

To this day, Horan describes that first lecture as one of the most important days of his life. It was his introduction to any form of Biblical prophecy, his first step on a journey that would ultimately lead him down a bizarre and controversial road.

Over the following months, Horan visited Barnett's house every Friday. The two grew close, drinking coffee and talking for hours about the contents of the Bible and what it all meant.

For months, Horan led a double life, slowly feeling his lifelong Catholic beliefs conflicting with what he was hearing inside the Fellowship.

Within weeks, Horan came clean with Barnett and the Fellowship about who he really was. But by the time he sat down to make his confession to Barnett, his cover was already blown. Unknown to Horan, Barnett and Hilsden had suspected from the very beginning that the young man who had walked in off the street into the Masonic Hall lecture was not a navvy working in Bexley.

His manner of speaking and familiarity with aspects of the Bible suggested that he was an educated young man and probably a man of religion of some sort. But what really gave Horan away were his hands. Hilsden worked in the plant-hire business and was familiar with the construction industry. He knew a navvy when he saw one and Horan just didn't fit the bill. He recalls that Horan's hands were far too 'smooth and clean' for a man supposedly mixing concrete and working with a shovel every day.

In fact, just weeks after his first arrival at the Fellowship, Hilsden's suspicions about Horan's real identity were confirmed.

Hilsden was standing at the counter of a fish-and-chip shop in Dartford. As he waited for his order, he peered out the front window and saw Horan getting off his bicycle. As Horan crossed the road to the chipper, he wrapped a scarf around his neck.

When Horan came inside, Hilsden greeted him and they spoke for a while. Anxious not to embarrass the priest, Hilsden did not mention that he had noticed his white collar as he got off his bike.

Horan continued to live a double life. On Sundays, he celebrated Mass in his parish church, only to cast his priestly collar aside later that evening to attend the Apostolic Fellowship lecture in Dartford. His curiosity about the Bible and his association with the Fellowship remained secret from his fellow priests as the Roman Catholic Church and the Fellowship held radically different views on many aspects of Bible teaching.

Horan began to accept the beliefs of the Fellowship and its members – the Fellowship's fundamental belief that the return of Christ would result in the establishment of a new kingdom where Jews would be gathered from all nations and restored to their own land, the principal dominion of Christ's new kingdom when he returned to earth.

The saints would not be reincarnated but raised from the dead on the return of Jesus to earth. They would act as servants, assisting Christ in his work, instructing the mortal population of the earth in God's laws. They would be teachers, leaders and rulers on behalf of Christ.

Horan was excited by the thought of this new kingdom and what it promised. A self-confessed melancholic, he was comforted to learn that under the rule of God's law in the new kingdom, conditions would improve for all, especially for those previously oppressed. Problems of famine and disease would diminish. Men and women would live longer but death would still feature for the thousand-year reign of this new world.

But the Fellowship's interpretation of certain aspects of the Bible placed Horan in a dilemma. The 'truths' he came to believe flew in the face of everything he had previously accepted as being true and right.

He began to question everything he and his family had previously accepted as truth. The Fellowship was effectively telling Horan that people like his Uncle John had simply got it wrong: 'When Rai told me the soul doesn't go to heaven when you die, that really shook me. That was a fundamental belief I grew up with. They told me there's no such thing as an immortal soul, that a person dies and is then as dead as a door nail.

'They were telling me that what I had believed up to then was all a false doctrine. Something kept telling me the Fellowship's beliefs can't be right.

'So where then are my forefathers gone? Are they dead in the grave, just like the animals? I was utterly shocked and thought, "This can't be right."

'I told Rai that he'd better have proof for all this in the Bible, and he did. And I also decided to find out for myself if all this was true by studying the Bible. And I did.' Over the next year, Horan's beliefs in some fundamental Catholic teachings were torn asunder. He came to believe that the fires of hell didn't exist, that canonising saints was a myth and the doctrine of the Trinity as taught by the Catholic Church was false.

In less than a year, Horan came to the conclusion that the Fellowship was right and the Catholic Church was wrong. The Bible was the proof and Barnett and Hilsden were able to use Scripture to back it all up.

At times, the new-found faith hurt Horan. If praying to the

dead or for the dead was a waste of time, so was praying to Our Lady, for she is also dead. This meant that the years on bended knee reciting the Rosary at home in Scartaglen, praying to Our Lady and praying for the dead, was futile nonsense.

In public, Horan continued to carry out his priestly duties. Privately, all his spare time was given over to studying the Bible and talking for hours with Hilsden and Barnett. They became friends, his teachers and family. The Fellowship had become Horan's new spiritual home and its members his siblings.

By Easter 1975, it was clear to Horan that he could no longer live a double life. He simply couldn't continue to preach one doctrine to his parishioners while believing something else.

His collar required him to ask people to believe in doctrines and follow religious practices he had come to believe were false and a total waste of time. He had to come clean.

Charles Henderson, Auxiliary Bishop of Southwark, agreed to Horan's request for a meeting. The bishop listened as his newest recruit told him he could no longer practise as a Catholic priest because his new-found beliefs and his association with the Apostolic Fellowship were totally at odds with Catholic teaching.

Henderson knew nothing of Horan's involvement with the Fellowship. But he did mention that a parishioner had written to him to complain that the local church was 'no longer Catholic'. Without fully realising it, Horan had begun to give parishioners selected insights into what he really believed. His Sunday sermons had become coloured by the beliefs of the Apostolic Fellowship.

The bishop scarcely responded to what Horan had to say, apart from telling him that some day he would come to regret the move. However, Horan was not for turning. He was walking out of his parish and would no longer practise as a priest. Days later, he packed his bags and left for Scartaglen. The parishioners in Bexley were told that Father Horan had left the parish for health reasons. Horan disappeared under a cloud of mystery.

At home in Scartaglen, Nellie and Free were glad to see their son coming home for what they believed was a well-deserved break.

That summer, Barnett and Jack Waller, another senior member of the Fellowship, arrived in Scartaglen. Introduced by Horan as 'two religious friends', they stayed for a week and chatted to the Horan family about God, the Jews and the second coming of Christ. Barnett and Waller were warm, courteous and articulate. Their faith clearly impressed the Horan clan. They did not mention anything about Horan leaving the priesthood. After a week in Scartaglen, they returned to Dartford. Soon after their departure, Nellie wrote a short letter to Barnett, thanking him and Waller for the visit and for a vice they sent from the UK that had arrived at Dublin Airport for use on the Horans' farm.

Nellie confirmed her promise that she too would study the Bible. She told Barnett how she and 'Path (sic) are making good progress with the reading' and 'every evening after the cows we do most of it'.

The weeks passed and Horan made no mention of going back to his parish. His holiday seemed suspiciously long. He had intended to tell his parents and family of his decision to quit, but the longer it went on the more difficult it seemed to become. He knew that leaving the priesthood would devastate his family and the entire parish. It was something that just wasn't done.

Nevertheless, Horan remained determined. He couldn't move on without first telling his family that he had done the unthinkable.

3

YOU'RE MAD AND YOU'RE FIRED

Nellie Horan buried her face in her hands and burst into tears. Free and Uncle Mike sat silent in shock. Embarrassed and ashamed, Neil waited for somebody to say something, anything, to help to ease the situation. He had told his closest family he had quit the priesthood. Getting kicked out of college was bad – walking out of the clergy was much worse.

The hours that followed Horan's announcement were awkward and quiet in the family home. For hours, nobody spoke to anybody. What Horan had just told his family was news they never wanted to hear. It was an affront to everything they wanted, believed and stood for. Horan had heaped shame on the family.

Late that night, Nellie eventually spoke to Neil: 'You didn't stay long, Neilie, did you?'

Her son did not answer. Glad that Nellie had broken the ice, Uncle Mike had his say too: 'Wasn't it awful for those two men from England to take a young garsún away from the priesthood?'

Horan believed his family knew full well what was going on. Despite the courteous welcome they had given Barnett and Waller just days before, he felt they must have known that Barnett and Waller were more than 'religious friends'.

For the first time, the pieces of the jigsaw appeared to be coming together. Barnett and Waller were surely too sweet to be wholesome. Now his parents believed the two to be members of a cult or sect that practised coaxing vulnerable and innocent young men like Horan away from their original Church of choice. Nellie remarked that Barnett and Waller must have been 'Jehobas' (sic) who had brainwashed her son into doing the unthinkable. Poaching Neil, a Catholic priest, was surely a trophy catch.

Family and friends feared that Horan would be ceremoniously paraded around Dartford by the Fellowship as the staunch Catholic priest who had converted to their beliefs.

The following day, Father Liam Dunne arrived at the Horan house in Scartaglen. He was a family friend and a relative through marriage, a highly regarded priest and a mild-mannered man. Father Dunne had been called to Scartaglen by the Horans in a desperate attempt to make sense of what had happened. More importantly, they hoped that Father Dunne could use his influence to talk sense to the young cleric who had surely lost his mind.

Horan was taken aback by Father Dunne's reaction to what had happened.

'Unlike me, my brother Pat was brave and challenged Father Liam because Pat too had studied the Bible. But as soon as he did, Father Liam turned to me and said I should be going down on bended knee and repenting for what I had done.

'It was worse than a death in the family. Time and again I was told to look at what I had done to my poor family, after all they had done for me. I told them I had left because of the truth.'

Horan left Scartaglen soon afterwards and returned to the UK. He left behind a family confused, angry and broken-hearted.

For the next six months, Barnett's house in the south of England was Horan's home. He grew closer to Barnett's religious group and in a swimming pool in Dartford, he was baptised as a brother in the Apostolic Fellowship.

No longer a practising priest, Horan secured a job as a storeman in Joyce Green Hospital in Dartford. It was a means to make a living and keep occupied, but every spare minute was devoted to studying the Bible.

Horan struggled to sever the spiritual ties he had with the Catholic Church. He had, after all, followed the script by getting ordained, finding a parish and settling relatively well into his life as a priest. For weeks, in Barnett's home, he wrestled with the notion that perhaps he had been duped by the Fellowship. Perhaps his vulnerability left him open to easy persuasion. The young cleric was a loner who had always found it hard to mix. In the Fellowship, he found a surrogate family who cared and looked out for him.

'Maybe I was naïve back then, coming from rural Ireland. But now, thirty-six years on, it's a different matter.

'I went to at least five other Churches and denominations including Mormons and Baptists, to compare them to the Fellowship in Dartford. My conclusion was the Fellowship got the whole thing right more than any of the others and had the evidence to back it up. Now, after all these years of study and tremendous research, I have never changed my views.'

At home in Scartaglen, moves were afoot to mend the damage. Horan's uncle, Father John, local members of the clergy and his own family concluded that Horan had been duped by a religious cult who took advantage of a mentally unstable young man. Father John wrote to his nephew, suggesting that the old problems he had experienced at Clonliffe College were back and that only a psychiatrist could sort it all out.

Horan resisted. At all times he insisted that he knew what he was doing. However, for the sake of peace with those he loved most, he said he'd go along with whatever they suggested.

Less than six weeks into his new job at the Joyce Green Hospital, Horan was summoned to the hospital administrator's office. He was told that his local GP, Dr Ghosh, had been in contact with the hospital after a meeting with his parents and the parish priest in Bexley.

After just one meeting with Horan, the GP told the hospital that Horan was mentally ill and could become violent. The hospital took Dr Ghosh's word. Horan was fired.

The move shocked Horan and infuriated Barnett and the Fellowship. They saw it as an attack on a man who was being punished because his views didn't conform with those of his family or with orthodox Catholic teaching. And an attack on Horan's beliefs was an attack on Barnett and the Fellowship.

Barnett went to work, lobbying politicians and corresponding with hospital management about their decision to fire Horan. He argued that Horan was perfectly stable mentally and the decision to terminate his employment was without reason or foundation.

Dr Howard Sergeant was regarded as one of the leading psychiatrists in London. He agreed to Barnett's request to carry out an independent assessment of Horan at his clinic in Harley Street. He examined Horan and reviewed his medical history.

Less than two months after Horan was fired, Dr Sergeant filed his first report: 'On the basis of my interview of Mr Horan, the additional information that I obtained from his friend who accompanied him (Rai Barnett) and my examination of Mr Horan, I consider that Mr Horan is not suffering from mental illness and that there is no psychiatric reason why he should not be employed in any work that his skills suit him for.' The report was totally at odds with what the hospital had been previously told by Dr Ghosh.

The hospital authorities, having admitted that Horan's dismissal had nothing to do with the standard of his work, were left red-faced. They had no choice but to accept Dr Sergeant's findings as he was a medical practitioner more qualified to comment on Horan's mental state than a local GP.

The Joyce Green Hospital authorities backed down and admitted they had got it wrong. Horan was taken back.

Desperate not to alienate his family for good, Horan began to try to explain in depth the situation that had arisen over previous years. He began with a letter to his brother Pat dated 14 February 1976:

> Dear Pat
>
> I have a lot of things to say and I think it would be too long if I tried to answer your letter now, but I will answer it in the near future...
>
> I am not saying for one minute that I was a perfect student in any of the places I attended. I was indeed far from it.
>
> Like Father Stephen [headmaster in Mount Melleray] said, I always was a bad mixer. I often broke the rules and wasted time doing useless things. I feel sure I was not as good as they say in the reports; they made me out to be a little better than I was...
>
> When Mam and Dad were here, they seemed sure that all the colleges sent out bad reports about my mental health to Father John. I could see this

made them upset and worry a lot worse for them. I want to do everything to lessen their sorrow.

So I wrote to all the seminaries, mostly for them, to try and clear up what was sent. I wrote to the seminaries too because I could not understand how they had left me go through and then turn around and say I was unbalanced...

I don't want to blame anyone. I don't want to blame Mam and Dad. I know they had no intention at all of getting me sacked.

I am not perfect, nor have I ever been. But I am not sick in my mind. I was not happy or discontented in Melleray or Wexford and neither was I in Bexley.

I know what I was doing when I left the Church. I left because and only because I believe the teachings of the Church are opposite to the Bible. I felt then, as I do now, that the Bible alone is the word of God.

I hope this information will help to ease the worry and trouble I have caused to all of ye. This is the only reason for sending it. It will not take away all the sorrow, but I hope it will take away some of it.

May the great God of heaven help and console all of ye. Best wishes,

Neilie

In a heartbreaking letter to Neil around the same time, Free Horan had asked his son numerous questions about the Fellowship and about God. In an eight-page reply to his father,

Neil explained why he had quit the priesthood and was devoting himself to the teachings of the Bible. With numerous quotations from the Scriptures, he tried to convince his father that what he had done was nothing to do with his mental state. His actions were all driven by his new-found religious beliefs.

> Dear Father
>
> At last I got around to answering the letter you wrote to me in January.
>
> You mentioned there is a veil over my eyes that I can't see through. We have no way of finding out what the ways of God are on our own.
>
> We are like helpless children. But the good God has told us what his ways are like a father would tell his children. He has given us the Bible. This book was given to take away the veil from people's minds. It was given to show them the true way, to be a light to lead them through this world of darkness.
>
> I think there was a veil over me until I started studying it. It has given me answers to questions that I had no idea how to answer in the past...
>
> You said you could not understand Rai's explanation about the Catholics bringing pagan practices down from pagan Rome, when his own father was a pagan who would listen to nobody.
>
> Rai's father was not a pagan, he was a Catholic and he believes in God. Rai often spoke to his father about the Bible but his father never agreed with him and never studied the Bible much.
>
> But surely what Rai's father believed has

nothing to do with what Rai believes. The father of the great Abraham was a pagan too, but Abraham was called to come away from his father's house...

You asked if I thought I had more wisdom than Sister Anthony. Of course not. Yes, she has a BA degree which I have not. She has given a long lifetime to teaching. As far as learning and wisdom are concerned, I do not compare with her. She had the experience of a long life while I have my little experience.

But the Bible says there is no need of great learning to understand it. In fact, it makes little of the learning and wisdom of the world and of what the world calls qualifications.

When Jesus went back to his own town of Nazareth after preaching in the rest of the country, this is what they had to say about him:

'Coming to his own country, he taught them in their synagogue, so that they were astonished and said, "Where did this man get his wisdom and these mighty works? Is not this the carpenter's son?"'

I am no one or nothing. Of myself, I know nothing about the ways of God. I am less clever than most people. But I can say that I have found in the Bible wonderful explanations of the ways of God.

I do not find it very hard to interpret. The main teaching of the Bible is that there will be a kingdom on the earth for 1000 years with Christ as King. When a person gets this right, all parts of the

Bible fit in with it…

Well, Dad, I hope these points help to answer your questions. If you have more, write to me and I will do my best to answer them.

May Jesus and our Heavenly Father guide ye all
Neilie

Horan's troubles appeared to subside. His family became resigned to the fact that the decision to hand in his resignation as a priest was more than a temporary blip. With his job back at the hospital and the support of the Fellowship nearby, Horan moved from Barnett's home and rented a small flat in Crayford, Kent. He remained extremely close to the Fellowship, attending their meetings and lectures at least three times every week. Stability had returned to his life, for a while at least.

Barnett had become a father figure to Horan. As an elder of the Fellowship group, Barnett had introduced him to the Scriptures. He and Jack Waller were the ones who travelled to Scartaglen to meet his parents when Horan was about to quit the priesthood. Barnett had taken Horan into his home when he had nowhere else to go. He was landlord, teacher and father in one.

But within five weeks of each other in the summer of 1976, Barnett and Waller both unexpectedly died. They were relatively young men and their deaths rattled all those close to them. Barnett's death in particular hit Horan harder than anything in his life up to then. The death of his mentor had an even greater impact than that of his sister Hannah.

By July 1979, the Fellowship was falling apart. The untimely deaths of the two elder members deeply affected the others in the Fellowship and had an adverse effect on the group's workings.

The internal wrangle in the Fellowship that culminated in

Derek Hilsden's decision to break away and form a new group called the Apostolic Ecclesia marked the beginning of the end of Horan's association with organised lectures on the Bible. The beliefs of the Apostolic Ecclesia were fundamentally identical to those of the Fellowship but the new group was missing some of Horan's close Fellowship friends.

Horan followed Hilsden but always believed that the split was unnecessary in the first place. Hilsden insisted that an issue of principle led to the departure of about twenty group members, far more than an internal power struggle or dispute. A senior member had decided to move with his family to another area for work reasons, without informing the group. Hilsden claims he and others who questioned the move were given an ultimatum either to 'accept what was done or leave the meetings'.

For Horan, the split appeared to be over a trivial issue, given the more 'serious matters' the group was all about. He was baffled as to why 'sincere Christians could fall out over one member'.

Friendships in the Fellowship ended, and with Barnett and Waller no longer there to steer the ship, Horan found himself lost at sea. Before long he quit the Apostolic Ecclesia.

Hilsden claims that Horan felt under pressure over his association with the new group, often being 'followed by members of the Catholic Church': 'I know that Neil struggled with the fact that only a small group of people held the same beliefs he did. He felt that thousands of people in the Catholic Church hadn't heard of any these things he had learned.

'He was determined to leave but I told him no matter what, if he ever needed me, I'd be there to see after him.' By 1979, Horan had left the group that had led him to throw off the Roman collar. The wandering days were back: he was on the road again.

4

A GLORIOUS NEW WORLD

Horan took a short break from his stroll around Belvedere Fort in Florence and sat on a vacant bench. He began to review the events of his life and think about where things should go from there. He had always dreamt of living in Italy one day and was fascinated by people like Michelangelo and Leonardo da Vinci. The Fellowship, too, had consistently placed emphasis on the Roman Empire.

Within weeks of his arrival in Trentino, Horan began to feel at home. With money saved, he had arranged his trip through an Italian woman who worked at Joyce Green Hospital and who was involved in a charity group that brought volunteers to various parts of her home country.

Horan didn't have a specific plan. He felt he could stay a year, maybe more, sightseeing and studying Italian history and culture. Most importantly, Italy was far away from his troubles in Dartford and Scartaglen.

Surrounded by the beauty of Belvedere, Horan began to hatch a new plan. Maybe time would heal the differences between him and the Catholic Church. Horan believed he had something to tell the world and that the knowledge he had gained from years of Biblical study was going to waste.

After arriving in Italy, he continued to study and pray and

still attended Sunday Mass. But he lacked an audience for what he had to say.

Having moved south to Florence from Trentino, Horan studied Italian every day and visited various historic sites. He found work as a kitchen porter in a small trattoria, quickly growing fluent in Italian and settling well among his new-found friends.

'For the last two months of my year in Italy, returning to the Catholic Church was uppermost in my mind. I thought to myself, "Why I am wasting my time here doing nothing with all I've learned?" I thought I could go back to the Church and preach the precious knowledge I had acquired.'

With nobody close enough to confide in, Horan decided to go straight to the hierarchy about his possible return to the Church.

The letter he penned to Charles Henderson, the Auxiliary Bishop of Southwark, appeared honest and frank. He told his superior he had thought everything over and wanted another chance.

But he deliberately made no mention of his desire to have it both ways – to use the Catholic pulpit to preach his own beliefs.

Bishop Henderson was delighted that Horan had come to his senses. He promptly replied to Horan, arranging a meeting for the prodigal son back in London with Michael Bowen, Archbishop of Southwark. After a year in Italy, Horan returned to the UK to further his plan.

Archbishop Bowen was impressed by Horan's honesty about the Fellowship and all that had happened in the previous years. Horan explained everything about his contact with the Fellowship, their basic beliefs and the reasons why he had walked out of his parish in Bexley without notice or explanation.

Before Horan could be reinstated, he needed to be cleansed. Like a man possessed, he needed to rid himself of everything he had come to believe over the previous six years and begin to think again like a normal Catholic priest. Once that was done, the whole incident could be passed off as a minor misunderstanding and a temporary spiritual deviation.

Of the twenty-two priests who attended the pastoral course in Stroud, Gloucestershire, Horan was the only one not an alcoholic. From June to Christmas of 1980, he sat among former clerical colleagues battling to recover from alcohol addiction. The course was run by the Paraclete Fathers and was based upon the principles of Alcoholics Anonymous and the twelve-step programme of recovery. Horan was sent there not to recover from alcohol or drug addiction, but to be reformed and rid of his heretical ways.

Every day, Horan listened to other priests confront their demons. Some confessed how they stole money from the church collection boxes to feed their habit; others admitted the shame of staggering drunk on to the altar to say Sunday Mass. 'I was made a sacristan at that course in Stroud simply because I wasn't an alcoholic. I think they looked at me as being potty, yet saw me as the only sane one around the place. I got the feeling they saw me as daft, as if I was some fella who believed in Santa Claus or a fairytale, something harmless and silly, something pie in the sky that was all based in the future. Looking back now, it amazes me they didn't pin me down more on my beliefs. I don't think they fully understood them.'

Horan was rigorously examined on what he had learned over the previous six years, but passed through his 'recovery' with flying colours.

His family was ecstatic at his decision to return to the Church.

Nellie and Free even made the trip to Stroud to visit their son. Neighbours and relatives around Scartaglen were told of Neil's miraculous recovery.

But members of the hierarchy in Southwark still weren't convinced. They believed that Horan needed to be further disinfected of all he had come to understand in the Dartford cult.

Horan agreed to a further five-month 'refresher' course in Rathgar, Dublin, before finally meeting all the requirements of his superiors. By May 1981, the troublesome cleric was cured at last. All had been forgiven. At no stage did Horan hint at his real motives for wanting to get back to preaching and what he planned to do when in the pulpit once more.

Events on the first day at his new parish in Plumstead, south-east London, didn't augur well. Horan hardly had his collar back on when news from the Vatican broke. Pope John Paul II had been shot by a Turkish gunman, narrowly escaping death.

For the two years after his reinstatement, the reformed cleric kept his beliefs to himself, ensuring that nothing except orthodox Catholic teaching found its way from the pulpit to the parishioners.

There was nothing sinister about the Church's decision to move him in 1983 to St Francis's parish in Clapham. It was part of a regular transfer of priests and Clapham became Horan's home for next five years, the longest period he would spend in any parish as a Catholic priest.

In the eyes of the Church and his parishioners, Horan was a good priest after he returned to the fold. Popular and hard-working, he strengthened links with other cultures by organising an Italian association while in Plumstead, often inviting the Scalabrinian Fathers to come and say Mass in the parish.

And he was making waves, too, among the most powerful

members of the Catholic Church. In 1983, Horan led a community group comprising Protestants and Catholics from Corrymeela, County Antrim, that had an audience with the Pope. Horan wore his kilt and danced in the Vatican, much to the amusement of Pope John Paul II. The Pope was oblivious to Horan's past, remarking after his jig that the dance was 'a great way to spread a message'.

Horan and his group were delighted with their visit to the Vatican and were met on their return by Archbishop Bruno Heim, the Papal Nuncio to Britain. The papers in London and Kerry splashed pictures of Horan and the Pope in full embrace at the Vatican.

While he ministered at St Francis's, Horan's parish cultural group made many plans. For two years, Horan and the group planned a trip to the Middle East, informing world leaders of their efforts to bring peace to the troubled land.

From Dublin, Taoiseach Charles Haughey wrote in response to news of the group's planned trip. Haughey sent warm greetings to 'those Irish who are so far away from their native land in the Middle East and the many friends of Ireland whom the touring party will meet during their visit.'

Tánaiste and Minister for Foreign Affairs Brian Lenihan also gave his blessing to Horan's project. In a letter sent in June 1987, Lenihan mentioned the Irish government's efforts, along with other countries of the European Community, to find a just and lasting settlement to the Arab-Israeli conflict. He wished Horan and his group 'every success in your worthwhile endeavours'.

But the trip never materialised: it was cancelled because of the volatile situation in the Middle East.

All the while, away from public scrutiny, Horan's opposition to Catholic teaching had become stronger than ever. The little spare time he had was devoted to writing in detail all he had learned since he first walked through the doors of the Masonic Hall in Dartford more than ten years before. Horan's writings – and their ultimate publication – would put the priest and the Catholic Church into a public stand-off and mark the beginning of the permanent end of Horan's association with Roman Catholicism.

The typed manuscript of his book, *A Glorious New World, Very Soon to Come*, made its way into the hands of Father Luke Verhes, the Dutch-born parish priest of St Francis's, when the printers sent it to the wrong address.

Verhes was alarmed at Horan's detailed explanations of Biblical prophecy. He informed Bishop Henderson, who immediately summoned Horan to a meeting to explain his latest antics.

Bishop Henderson did not consider himself qualified to deal with what Horan had written. The lengthy document dealt with complex interpretations of scriptural prophecies. He referred the manuscript to Father John Redford, a scholar of scripture based in the diocese. Father Redford conveyed his opinion of the book to the bishop, stating that he and the Catholic Church fundamentally disagreed with Horan's interpretations of prophecies.

The bishop believed that if he could make sure that the book wasn't published for a mass audience, this would ensure that little harm could be done. He ordered that only twenty-five copies of the book be printed. But Horan's printer advised him that producing such a small quantity would be uneconomical. Horan had four hundred copies printed.

The two-hundred-and-seventy-page hardback was dedicated to members of Horan's family and the people of Scartaglen:

parents Free and Nellie, Father John, Auntie Nora, Auntie Bride and Sister Anthony. The dedication read: 'They gave excellent examples to me of living the faith. I pray that I may never betray that faith, which they and so many other good people have helped to give me.'

In the opening lines of *A Glorious New World*, Horan introduces himself as 'a weak and unimportant human being'. However, the book's contents, he argues, are of 'high and mighty importance to every one of you'.

If his outline of the future of the world and its people were proven wrong, he wrote, then God would be his judge.

The entire book is based on the premise that the 'golden age of the whole world is very near' and will 'come to all religions and races through one small country, Israel'.

Horan wrote that the Israelites would be God's chosen people, 'despite all their many failures and failings': 'God was entitled to choose whoever He wished, and He freely picked the Jews to bring salvation and happiness to the ends of the earth.'

The book has Israel as its centre and main theme. 'Unless we are totally mistaken, the rebirth of Israel in 1948 was the greatest event in the whole history of the world.'

Horan claims one of the most central messages of the Bible was clear and unambiguous: God promised Abraham that he would live forever in the 'Promised Land'. His 'seed' – the Jewish people who descended from him – received the same promise.

Horan says the promise was clear. 'What other possible meaning can we make out of it? If we do not believe what it says, we surely make God a liar. He would not have promised something and not carried out that promise.'

Horan wrote at length about the Jews. He would continue to write numerous articles about them in the years that followed, describing them as arch-villains – 'arrogant, suspicious, narrow, corrupt and boastful'. But his argument has always been that their present wickedness is irrelevant; what really matters is that they are the chosen people and what is to happen when Christ returns. After they have been 'purged at Armageddon…the Jews will never again fail in their great calling'.

At no point in *A Glorious New World* does Horan challenge the validity of other religions. On the contrary, he encourages members of other religions to be more loyal and devoted to their own beliefs.

He explains the origins and main message of all the main religions: Jewish, Christian, Muslim, Hindu, Jain, Sikh, Buddhist, Confucian, Taoist and Shinto.

Despite the fact that Biblical writings originate from numerous authors over a period of 1500 years, Horan argues the unity on major themes is 'striking'.

Some of the Bible is symbolic or figurative, so those symbols can only be understood by exploring what they meant to the Jewish people at the time they were written.

As Horan had learned from Barnett and Hilsden in the Fellowship, he says that words like 'heaven', 'earth', 'air', 'sun', 'moon' and 'stars' have a meaning beyond the literal.

Horan claims these words are used in the prophecies as descriptions of 'distinct classes of rulers or leaders', while 'heaven' refers to 'all classes together'.

It was Horan's interpretation of signs that the coming of Christ is near that put his beliefs significantly at odds with the teaching of the Catholic Church.

An entire section of the book focuses on Russia's future role in the world's end; how the modern world has been shaped by the French Revolution and how the fall of the Turkish empire left Palestine free to become Israel. The book also deals at length with the future roles of Britain, Russia, Ethiopia, Iran (Persia), Egypt, Saudi Arabia, Jordan, Lebanon, Iraq, Syria and Libya.

Horan claims that the speed and scope of progress and development on earth, particularly since about 1800, clearly point to the inevitable fact that the end is near.

> (Man) has conquered the mighty waves; he has climbed the highest mountains; he has gone to the depths of the deepest seas; he has dug deep into the earth and brought out its treasures, which was his right; he can talk to his fellow man on the other side of the globe; he has conquered the air, he can fly through it...his skill and intelligence have mastered this planet, so much so he is starting to go out to other planets.

At the end of the book, Horan claims that the Antichrist will appear. He asks: 'Who will the Antichrist actually be?' but does not answer this question.

Instead he says, 'We must all pray for guidance from God to help us to arrive at the answer. We must pray that when the real Christ does come, we will recognise him as the true Son of God.

'There is a danger that some will mistake the real Christ and think he is the Antichrist. There is an equal danger that some will mistake the Antichrist and think he is the real Christ.'

Despite this, Horan's book concludes that Christ, the Messiah, 'will come for all religions and peoples. He will fulfil the prophecies of Michael Nostradamus, of Jeane Dixon, of Edgar Cayce and of Fatima.'

In its final message, *A Glorious New World* emphatically

predicts 'great and wonderful blessings will arrive on earth with Jesus' return, and those will come from Jerusalem and the Jews. Only then will Jesus explain 'why God chose the Jews in the first place'.

Horan's theory of the second coming can be summarised as Christ ruling the world from Jerusalem. There will be two classes of people: 'Immortal saints' who will rule a world government for 1000 years from Jerusalem, and 'mortal citizens' who will become adopted Jews and live for 900 years.

Horan easily found a home for each of the four hundred copies of his book. He had a summary of the book translated into Arabic and sent to twenty-seven Arab leaders of various countries, among them King Fahd, President Assad, Colonel Ghadaffi and President Saddam Hussein.

In the years that followed, Horan would receive numerous responses from world leaders, all of them thanking him for sending a copy of his book.

Michael Alison, parliamentary private secretary of the British Prime Minister Margaret Thatcher, wrote to tell Horan that the Prime Minister thanked him for 'your most interesting book and other references to your sterling and imaginative efforts in the cause of promoting world peace'.

Years later, Prime Minister Tony Blair's private secretary, Sandra Philips, would tell Horan that Mr Blair was 'most grateful' for the book.

The Thai embassy in London wrote to Horan, telling him the ambassador found the book 'of considerable interest, blending as it skilfully does, a factual presentation of the religions of the world with the message...of their movement towards the focal point in Israel'. The embassy even announced its intention to make the book available to Thai people.

Towards the end of Horan's term in Clapham, his sermons from the altar had begun to change direction and emphasis. Whenever he could, he'd preach to parishioners about the Jews and the prophecies and how Israel would again become a great nation.

He managed to steer clear of the more controversial aspects of his beliefs and nobody seemed to object to Father Neil. After all, he was a good priest and was doing good work. His first substantial piece of writing had been published without any drastic consequences.

But *A Glorious New World* was merely a taste of what was to come. The Catholic hierarchy and the parishioners had seen nothing yet.

5

LIVE TV

Horan couldn't muster the courage to tell Father Verhes to his face and he certainly couldn't tell the bishop or the parishioners. Instead, on a May morning in 1988, he left a note on a table of the presbytery at St Francis's parish addressed to his parish priest. In it he explained the peace jig he planned to do outside the BBC studios in London, followed by a peace tour of Northern Ireland.

But the last line of the note told of something Horan had done before: he was walking out of the priesthood again.

Ever since his return from Italy, Horan had wanted to use the collar and the pulpit to preach his beliefs. However, so far his diversions from orthodox Catholic teaching had been relatively few and mild.

Apart from the publication of his book, *A Glorious New World*, the unconventional cleric rarely came to the attention of his superiors. What he really believed in the privacy of his own mind and heart was irrelevant, as long as that was where his beliefs remained. The preceding years had been happy and Horan appeared to have settled down for the first prolonged period of his life.

Now it was different. For the first time, he wanted to go public with his views. His actions would undoubtedly cause consternation and probably lead to his dismissal from the

Church. Well aware of the potential consequences, Horan was determined to push ahead. This time, he would quit the priesthood and go on a mission to publicise the Bible, performing his Irish jig and distributing leaflets in the hope of spreading his message to those who bothered to look or ask, as well as winning the attention of the mass media.

The morning he left the handwritten note, he spoke briefly to Bishop Henderson who had telephoned him after hearing about the planned 'peace dance' outside the BBC. The bishop wanted to meet Horan, but the curate told him he couldn't make the appointment.

The decision to leave St Francis's parish is one Horan regrets to this day. It was, he says, a 'rash decision, almost irresponsible, leaving without even saying goodbye to your colleagues'.

That morning, probably for the first time, Horan began to see things from the Church's perspective. The second, third and fourth chances, the 'refresher' courses and treatment centres – they would all count for nothing: 'I could well understand the hierarchy saying at that time, "Let's wash our hands of him," justified in saying, "We have enough of this lunatic." Yet to be fair to them they didn't do that.'

For a full week, Horan arrived every day outside the BBC studios in Wood Lane in west London. Dressed in a cream kilt, green jacket and knee-high green socks, the curate from Clapham danced a jig in the full glare of the public.

By doing the bizarre, he hoped to catch the attention of some journalist or producer inside, or at least let the media know that he was in town. Between the jigs, Horan distributed leaflets to passers-by, explaining the prophecies of Jeremiah and Isaiah and the history of the Jews.

The BBC didn't bite but some media did.

At home in Kerry, Horan made the front page of his local newspaper, *The Kerryman*. He was quoted extensively, calling on Taoiseach Charles Haughey, British Prime Minister Margaret Thatcher and Queen Elizabeth to be ready to lead their people should the end of the world arrive during their terms in office.

In his local newspaper, the *South London News*, the photo caption read, 'The lord of the dance'.

The peace dance outside the BBC studios was the first time Horan really came under the public spotlight. But what appeared to intrigue people and the media the most was not Horan's message of the second coming. Instead, it was the fact that a forty-one-year-old priest, dressed in a kilt, was dancing a jig to promote his message about the end of the world.

Horan had a reason for wearing his 'national costume' while performing a peace jig. He wanted to 'pay tribute to the cultures of all nations and peoples, in particular their gifted musicians, singers and dancers'. Irish dancing was an integral part of his childhood growing up in Sliabh Luachra and the kilt was part of the costume worn by many boy dancers.

Horan also wished to model himself on King David. By wearing the star of David on his costume, he wanted to identify with David's throne from which, he believed, Christ would reign after the second coming.

The harp on his costume was worn as the national emblem of Horan's native country. It was also the instrument played by King David, also believed to be a dancer and the composer of many of the psalms.

But the most controversial part of Horan's costume at every public appearance would prove to be his green silk underpants, or 'knickers' as Horan calls them. In defence of wearing his short kilt and 'green knickers', Horan would argue years later that men, just as women, were entitled to wear what they like.

'It should not be all about women getting their rights,' he said. 'In some cases, it is men who need rights. I demand the same rights regarding my form of dress as if I were female. The young women in Riverdance wear very short skirts and there is nothing about it.'

The first real taste of publicity from his week-long demonstration outside the BBC studios spurred Horan on.

He returned home to Scartaglen, telling his parents that he had landed himself in trouble with the bishop but would return to his priestly duties in the near future.

With that, he set off on a tour to Northern Ireland, stopping first at Dáil Eireann in Dublin. The political establishment was clearly unaware of who Horan was or what he was about. Outside the Dáil, Alan Dukes, the leader of Fine Gael, the main opposition party, met the touring priest and accepted a copy of his book, *A Glorious New World*.

Horan cycled onwards north, stopping in each major city and town to perform his jig and to distribute leaflets.

In Belfast, he had more than a dozen meetings with top political and security figures. He met Ian Paisley, then leader of the Democratic Unionist Party (DUP), as he left a church having listened to him preach. Former Ulster Volunteer Force (UVF) leader and convicted murderer, Gusty Spence, also listened to the priest's views on the end of the world.

The Catholic priest danced his way down the hardline loyalist Shankill Road, Spence's birthplace.

At the headquarters of the Royal Ulster Constabulary (RUC), Assistant Commissioner Wilson and seven top RUC officers accepted Horan's gift of a picture of a menorah, one of the oldest symbols of the Jewish faith.

For Horan, the publicity trip was a success. Local newspapers and Ulster TV pictured Horan dancing his way round Belfast. Curiosity was aroused.

But by May of 1989, Horan's publicity mission had taken its toll. His cycle tour of Northern Ireland took him from a personal high to feeling tired and low. He went back to Dublin to meet a psychiatrist. This time, he was referred to St John of God's Hospital in Dublin for six weeks of residential care.

At last, the medical profession appeared to be getting to grips with what was going on inside Horan's head.

Psychologists reported on a man they deemed to be psychotic and suffering from obsessional tendencies. One report described him as a quiet man who did not engage in any 'spontaneous conversation as he appeared quite depressed'.

Horan's overall level of function was described as lying within the average range of intellectual ability. But this masked a 'rather uneven performance', which was lowered by anxiety and 'obsessional behaviour'.

The dancing priest was found to be introspective, obsessional in his thinking and behaviour and ruminative, lacking in self-confidence, self critical, self-conscious, self-degrading and plagued by self-doubts.

Horan admitted then, and he still does, that he suffered from depression. He claimed the condition was intensified around this time due to the death of his mother. But he was happy to go along with whatever the doctors said of him.

Although fully aware of what the medical profession had found, the Church refused to wash their hands of Horan. Again they allowed him back, despite his walking out on his parish on two occasions and dancing his way around Ireland in a kilt.

His superiors sent him for another six-month 'refresher

course', this time at a Benedictine abbey in Kent. Again, Horan appeared to be stable and to pose no further threat or embarrassment.

By March 1990, the dancing priest had the collar back on, taking temporary posts in Birchington, Kent, and Wimbledon. But four months into an appointment in Anerley in south-east London, Horan was back at his old tricks, openly preaching his beliefs from the pulpit.

According to Horan, a fellow-cleric wrote to the bishop, warning that the troublesome priest's sermons had taken a 'dangerous turning', often delving more into world politics than the word of the Gospel. Worse still, his colleague complained that Horan's sermons had become long and boring.

Bishop Henderson again summoned Horan, but this time the solution would be different. Psychiatric treatment hadn't seemed to work, so the Church authorities relied on another tried and tested solution. He was moved to another parish – St Thomas's in Nunhead, closer to central London.

The apparent reluctance of the Church to deal with him definitively by kicking him out almost amused Horan. Even now, he wryly smiles at the decision of his superiors to move him to another parish: 'Sure moving me wasn't going to solve the problem at all. I can see the comparison people might make with a child sex abuse case. It's almost disturbing and uncanny.'

Over the next three years, parishioners at St Thomas's grew to like their new priest. Whatever Horan's eccentricities or beliefs, he was always courteous and kind. To some, his personal history up to then was that of a man psychiatrically ill, unsettled and downright odd. For others, it appeared that Horan had something interesting to say, if only people would listen.

Life had dealt its fair share of knocks to Horan and his

family. In 1992, another blow was dealt when he lost his younger brother. Denis Horan never walked or spoke. He was severely physically and intellectually disabled from birth and shortly after Hannah's tragic death in 1968, went into full-time care at St Mary of the Angels in Beaufort, a residential centre run by the Franciscan nuns.

Denis's death on 25 September 1992, at the age of just twenty-eight, did not come as a complete shock to the Horan family, as few had expected him to live a long life. His parents and siblings regularly visited him in Beaufort, but according to Neil, nobody really had a close relationship with Denis. He rarely recognised any of his family and appeared completely unaware of his surroundings.

'In one way, we were almost glad he had found peace when he passed on. It was also a release for my father and family because all of us found it hard seeing him, knowing he never recognised any of us. But the family always accepted it. It was nobody's fault.'

At Denis's funeral Mass in Scartaglen, Neil drew on his knowledge of the Bible and its references to the marginalised and the weak.

Later that day, two of the sisters from St Mary of the Angels called to the Horan home in Knockeenahone. One of them, Sr Maura, had looked after Denis for eighteen years. She told Free how she often played the accordion for Denis, and when she went to put the instrument back in its box, Denis would tug at her sleeve as if to signal he wanted to hear more.

This came as a surprise to the Horan family who had always believed Denis was oblivious to what was going on around him. And it came as some consolation, too, to know that he found enjoyment from music during his time in care.

Back in Nunhead, Horan's popularity grew. His supporters

were gaining momentum, enough at least for a group of parishioners to publish a forty-six page booklet entitled *Father Neil Horan's Life and Works and His Present View of World Events*.

The ten signatories at the back of the booklet claimed that they were greatly impressed by Horan's weekly column in the parish magazine and that Horan's book, *A Glorious New World*, should be reissued because of 'overwhelming' demand.

The signatories to the booklet claimed that Horan's own book was 'quite simply one of the most awesome and inspiring books ever written'. They claimed that they were publishing the booklet because they had some 'time to spare' between them, whereas there was 'no way Father Neil would have the time to do so, at least while he is in our parish'.

The booklet quoted Horan extensively: his outline of how Russia would play a central role in the Muslim invasion of Israel that would kick-start the third World War and signal Armageddon. On the other side, according to Horan, would be 'English–speaking countries' comprising Britain, America, Canada, Australia and New Zealand.

Along with brief background information on the parish and a history of Horan's own life and family history, the booklet detailed Horan's beliefs on prophecy. It was effectively the written Gospel according to Neil Horan.

With the aid of supporters and parishioners, Horan did relaunch an updated version of his book in 1992. Since he first published it seven years previously, its circulation had been limited to four hundred copies. Copies of the new edition were sent to world leaders and embassies, including the Embassy of the Russian Federation, the Kenyan High Commission, Buckingham Palace and the White House.

The international community appeared to receive Horan's

book particularly well. Letters of congratulations and appreci-
ation were sent by people from Sri Lanka, India, the Carribean,
the Philippines, Africa and the Czech Republic.

Horan reflected on how the majority of people who had
received copies of his book and wrote to him were practising
Catholics. He claimed that the letters of support showed 'the
extraordinary things that can be done by ordinary people':

'All the writers are simple, common people. None of them
have college education. Some are foreigners, whose English is
not great in conversation. Yet, with all these letters, I was amazed
at how well the writers expressed themselves – far better than I
would have thought possible beforehand.'

With a book under his belt, a weekly column in the parish
magazine, a booklet written about his life and his beliefs, free
rein at the altar and regular appearances in the local press,
Horan's profile was on the rise.

An invitation in 1993 to dance a jig on *Kenny Live*, the prime-
time television show in Ireland, was music to Horan's ears.
Programme researchers visited Scartaglen and his appearance
was scheduled but it never came to pass.

His superiors and family were willing to tolerate the publicity
up to now, but live TV was a step too far and a risk too great.
After the programme's staff made contact, the Catholic hierarchy
in Britain issued an ultimatum to Horan: 'Appear on TV with Pat
Kenny and you're out for good.' Horan was furious. He knew that
the appearance on prime-time television in Ireland would have
been priceless. In any event, their contact with the hierarchy and
the advice Church bosses offered about Horan's mental health
resulted in programme bosses pulling the plug on the interview.

Gutted at the lost chance, Horan refused to back down. This
time, he began to challenge those who questioned his mental

health. Speculation about his health was based on hearsay, he argued, always linked to his public profile, never to his beliefs.

Immediately after the TV appearance that never was, Horan wrote to Dr Des McGrath, the first psychiatrist he had consulted when he was a student way back in 1967, the same specialist who referred him to St John of God's in 1989. He told Dr McGrath that his original psychiatric report in 1967 had remained with him 'like an albatross around my neck' and he demanded a short report on any mental illness he had.

Dr McGrath refused to supply a medical opinion. He claimed that giving labels to psychiatric disorders 'can be very misleading and can rarely be adequately described in a sentence'. In 1989 Dr McGath had written to Horan's bishop, advising that Horan would only be capable of working as a priest under 'close supervision'.

Horan also wrote to Dr Mary Clarke-Finnegan, a consultant psychiatrist who had seen him in 1989. He told her of his disgust that the issue of his mental health was now being used against him at every opportunity. He requested a letter to explain her diagnosis.

According to Horan, nobody had yet come forward to state clearly what was so wrong with him that it had become a major point of concern and kept him off the TV.

Like Dr McGrath, Dr Clarke-Finnegan refused to accede to Horan's request. In her letter of reply dated March 1994 she noted his 'dissatisfaction at the apparent interference by your family with your plans to appear on *Kenny Live*'. But she told the priest that having a letter from her, commenting either positively or negatively on his mental health, would not be in his best interests. She claimed that if she issued such a letter it would be wide open to misinterpretation out of context. In any event, five years had passed since she had last seen Horan and any medical opinion would be rendered invalid.

Horan eventually gave in. The persistent references to his mental health by his colleagues in the priesthood and family in Scartaglen led to his agreeing to be assessed one more time.

He acceded to a request from his parish priest, Father Jeff Cridland, to return home to Ireland for further psychiatric examination. Without any formal farewell, Horan left his parish in Nunhead and flew to Ireland. He would never again return to active ministry in the Catholic Church.

6

OH YES HE'S MAD, OH NO HE'S NOT

'Armageddon priest is barred by parish'. The *Daily Telegraph* headline caught Derek Hilsden's eye. Hilsden read on. The man he had befriended sixteen years earlier in the Fellowship in Dartford had been expelled from his parish in Nunhead for proclaiming a 'nuclear Armageddon and the second coming of Christ'.

Hilsden was intrigued but worried. He had promised Horan the day he left the Apostolic Ecclesia, sixteen years earlier, that if he ever needed help, he would be there to give it.

Through the *Telegraph*'s Religious Affairs Correspondent, Damian Thompson, Hilsden tracked down his old friend who was staying in community accommodation run by a lay Christian group in Baldock, Hertfordshire. The psychiatric assessment at home in County Kerry had concluded that Horan would be better off staying in some form of sheltered accommodation in the UK, out of the priesthood and out of harm's way.

Hilsden left a business card at the address and Horan rang back later that evening. Concerned for his wellbeing, Hilsden agreed to meet Horan that night underneath a motorway bridge near Luton. His recollection of that evening is one that remains clear in his mind to this day.

'The moment I met him I knew he was not right. He was in a

real state. I believed he was on the verge of a breakdown.

'He had a little old bag and his vest was on outside his shirt. He was unhygienic and he had not looked after himself at all. I invited him to stay with our family and he rang the following day to take up the offer.'

For the next year, Horan stayed in the Hilsden home. His departure from the priesthood and the public controversy that ensued was taking its toll.

For the first five weeks in his new home, Horan rarely left his dark bedroom, except to join Hilsden and his wife for meals. He appeared untidy and unhygienic and oblivious of money matters. Hilsden refused to take any rent and helped the priest out with the few small bills he had.

Meanwhile, the debate about Horan's departure from his parish in Nunhead raged in the media.

Throughout 1994, national and local newspapers in the UK and Ireland regularly reported on a mad priest who had been banished from his parish because of his heretical views on the end of the world.

For several months, it was one-way traffic. The Church hierarchy remained silent, refusing to be drawn into a doctrinal debate. Only one version of the story ever appeared to get oxygen and that was Horan's.

He persistently presented himself as the victim, claiming that he had been banished from the parish because his religious views differed from Catholic teaching.

In August of 1994, his former parish priest, Father Jeff Cridland, stepped into the fray. Father Cridland cared a great deal for Horan but had previously described Horan's beliefs as 'complete and utter tosh'.

Father Cridland had also written to Horan, telling him he

had enough to do in the parish and to get over the death of a priest friend, 'without having a priest in my house who is in controversy with the Archbishop'. He asked Horan to stay away from Nunhead until the controversy was resolved and to 'refrain from returning unannounced'.

But in August 1994, after a spate of newspaper articles, Father Cridland went public in defence of Horan and to set the record straight. He told the *Cork Examiner* newspaper that allegations of Horan being 'banished' from the parish were untrue.

'Father Horan is a lovely person. He certainly did not air his views from the pulpit and we never said he could not preach,' Father Cridland told the newspaper. 'Nobody else has asked me about him. Despite this the media is saying we fell out over his beliefs about Armageddon. It is not true and his family know it. He did not preach about it.

'Some reports have implied I said his preaching was heretical and that I told him to stop. This did not happen and there was no conflict between us over his sermons.'

The Southwark diocese backed Father Cridland's public intervention. Father Richard Moth, a diocese spokesman, admitted that some of Horan's theories had caused consternation, but Father Cridland and Horan had reached an 'amicable agreement'.

The public debate appeared to boil down to one question captured in a headline in a Kent newspaper: 'Mad – or right to say what he believes?'

The writer argued that the big question for Neil Horan was whether he should see a psychiatrist. According to the article, other questions about the end of the world and the second coming were not so crucial for him at that time.

Horan was described in the article as 'impossibly vulnerable'.

'His head is too big for his body, his hair is dead black and his eyes are almost hidden behind thick-rimmed glasses.'

Back in Nunhead, Father Cridland was left to pick up the pieces. A group of about forty parishioners wrote letters to newspapers in support of the priest they believed had been unfairly stripped of his collar. In a statement issued to the media, the support group pleaded with Church authorities to bring the cleric back: 'Please take Neil back and allow him to continue to claim his prophecies, by all means. It seems to us he is one of the few Catholic priests anywhere in the world who is openly proclaiming the prophecies. He is clearly an expert on the subject and has a great ability to explain it. Could history yet judge him a chosen servant of God for these last days?'

The group said it considered Horan to be of sound mind, despite the view being 'widely circulated around Nunhead over the last five months that he is mentally ill and we strongly disagree with this view.'

Support for Horan was not confined to parishioners and friends. The Christadelphians, a religious group that bases its beliefs entirely on the Bible, also rallied to the priest's side, writing several letters of disgust at the Catholic Church's decision to cut ties with the priest, simply for believing what they felt was the truth.

Many of them had read newspaper articles that told how Horan was 'banished' from his parish. They argued that what Horan believed was not, in fact, 'complete and utter tosh' as had been suggested by Father Cridland.

Among the letters of support was one from a Mrs K. L. Holman from West Sussex:

Dear Neil Horan

I read with great interest the article in the *Daily Telegraph* which referred to you as being 'banished' for your beliefs in the Bible and its clear teaching.

You are of course totally correct in your belief and understanding of the return of Jesus Christ to the earth, the 1000-year reign of Jesus Christ on the earth and the establishment of the Kingdom of God on earth, with Jerusalem as its capital.

All of which you correctly state is shown in the Scriptures to be the ultimate purpose of God, signs of which include the return of the Jews to their land, and in other fulfilled prophecies, and the as yet unfulfilled prophecy of *Ezekiel* 38, concerning the invasion of Israel from a northern confederacy, which we as Christadelphian Bible students believe to be Russia.

Christadelphians have believed and taught all of the above since our pioneer brethren revived the truth of the Scriptures in about 1848.

The Churches have corrupted and apostatised those truths, and have led many into error. Hence our obedience to the word of God recorded by the Apostle Paul in 2 *Corinthians* 6: 17-18: 'Wherefore come out from among them (the apostasy), and be ye separate, saith the Lord, and touch not the unclean, and I will receive you, and I will be a father unto you, and ye shall be my sons and daughters, saith the Lord almighty.'

Similar words can be found in *Revelation* 18: 4. I have included a pamphlet or two that you may find of interest. There are many more which help to uncover the glorious truth of the Scriptures, as they are entirely scripturally based, and form the basis of our lives as Bible students.

What a sad reflection that you have been considered mentally ill for exposing the doctrine of the word of God which is supposed to be the basis of Christian faith.

Your 'banishment' article has highlighted the very subject spoken of at Christadelphian Bible lectures held all over the country, and abroad, each Sunday.

May it be that you will be able to pursue your belief, God willing, with those you have been able to enlighten.

There are a number of Christadelphians who were once Catholics. If we can in any way assist you, please do let us know.

The debate about Horan wasn't confined to the media and the parish. Members of the psychiatric profession too were at odds over a clear diagnosis.

Despite the public spat, Father Cridland remained supportive of his former curate, convinced that psychiatric treatment was the only way forward. He brought Horan to see Dr Mark Blackwell, a consultant psychiatrist based at Greenwich District Hospital. After a lengthy meeting with Horan and Father Cridland in September 1994, Dr Blackwell forwarded a detailed report of what he found to Horan's doctor.

According to the psychiatrist, Horan eventually accepted the concerns raised by those close to him that he had a personal hygiene problem, after initially explaining it as a result of having come from a farming background.

He was 'keen to put his side of what he thought was a dispute over his sanity and accusations of him suffering from schizophrenia or a schizophrenic tendency,' the report said.

Dr Blackwell found the priest to be smartly turned out and not suffering from depression. Neither did he show signs of thought disorder. However, he found Horan's 'disastrous relationships with friends, relatives, colleagues and jobs to be so consistent and persistent that they do constitute evidence of abnormality'.

'His lack of self-care on occasion to the point of being so smelly it becomes a problem for those who live with him and his withdrawal into his own room and bizarre behaviour and ideas would all fit with the diagnosis of schizophrenia.' Dr Blackwell went on to say there was no evidence of schizophrenia 'on talking to him', but it was the 'most probable diagnosis'.

However, in a letter sent directly to Horan three weeks later, Dr Blackwell made no mention of schizophrenia. Instead, he wrote that Horan was suffering from a 'biological disorder of brain function'.

The psychiatrist sought more background information over the following weeks and promised to prescribe an anti-psychotic drug if his opinion did not change.

Horan was furious at Dr Blackwell's view and Hilsden also disagreed with the diagnosis. In fact, Hilsden wrote to the psychiatrist, painting a completely different picture of Horan.

According to Hilsden, the suggestion of Horan's mental illness originated from 'some misguided attempt by members of his family to undermine his confidence in his new religious persuasion'. Hilsden argued there was no mental or physical problem. Horan's troubles were of a spiritual nature. His friend was suffering from a troubled conscience from trying to 'reconcile the irreconcilable when he finds his understanding of the Bible is not accepted nor encouraged by his superiors'.

Desperate for another opinion, Horan returned to Dr Howard Sergeant, the psychiatrist who first saw him in 1975. Dr Sergeant's diagnosis in 1994 was the same as his earlier one and was totally at odds with Dr Blackwell's view.

According to Dr Sergeant, 'Father Horan's problem seems to me to be a spiritual one, with a conflict inherent in his spanning a spectrum of views from Roman Catholicism on one hand and the more evangelical Apostolic Ecclesia on the other.'

Dr Sergeant pointed out that 'having convictions or even unconventional beliefs is not necessarily a symptom of mental illness'. He said he found no evidence that Horan suffered from an obsessive compulsive disorder.

If the controversial priest possessed a number of obsessional traits, Dr Sergeant regarded these as 'helpful to his working to high standards rather than a hindrance'. Nor did Horan require any medication.

Unsurprisingly, Horan saw it Dr Sergeant's way when it came to his mental state. By the following month, the Kerryman had enough of Dr Blackwell and Dr Blackwell had enough of the heretic priest.

In an angry letter to Horan's GP, Dr Blackwell reported on another long meeting he had with his patient.

He remarked that since their previous meeting, the priest had 'managed to get two articles about himself, one in the *Daily Telegraph* and one in the *Catholic Herald*, both of them accusing the Catholic hierarchy of booting him out and gagging him'.

He complained that Horan had taken one of the doctor's confidential letters about his illness around to people, obtaining psychiatric, sociological and theological opinions on it. 'All of them have been critical of me,' Dr Blackwell wrote.

He described Horan's manner on the day of his examination as being 'querulous, irritable, accusatory, dismissive, ironic and downright paranoid on occasions... He seemed to feel it was perfectly reasonable to attack one's doctor in public as he feels he himself is under attack.'

Dr Blackwell sought an assurance from Horan that his name would not appear in the newspapers or on television. Horan refused to give him this assurance. Dr Blackwell told the GP that he had recommended to Horan that he go back to St John of God's for treatment for schizophrenia.

By the end of 1994, Horan had emerged from the darkness of his bedroom in Hilsden's home and was back studying the Bible and actively promoting his interpretations of the Scriptures.

After his intense engagement with psychiatrists, he was more convinced than ever that his convictions and the lengths to which he was willing to go to proclaim them were being misdiagnosed as mental illness. And he had support for his stance, not least from his former brothers in the Apostolic Ecclesia.

Hilsden and his group organised a public meeting in Peckham, south London, entitled 'Towards Armageddon'. It was sparked primarily by the controversy surrounding Horan's departure from the Church. About sixty-five people turned out to hear Hilsden give a lengthy lecture on Bible prophecy.

Hilsden explained that the meeting had been 'occasioned by reports in the national and local press about the views of the curate of Nunhead and the disapproval of his superiors in the Catholic Church leading to his suspension'.

He prefaced his lecture by saying that the controversy in the parish of Nunhead had wider implications than just a disagreement between a curate and his parish priest and that this was a matter of greater concern than Horan's mental health. The whole issue, according to Hilsden, was 'clearly a question of conflict of doctrine'.

Over the next hour at the public meeting, Hilsden argued that remarkable political events that were shaping the world were more than coincidental. The end of the Cold War, the fall of communism, the disintegration of the Soviet Union, the reunification of Germany, majority rule in South Africa and the peace process in the Middle East had transformed the world political scene.

But the changes had not made the world a safer place. Natural disaster, political instability, civil wars, famines, the rise of fundamentalism and the threat of the uncontrolled spread of nuclear weapons were diminishing people's confidence in the ability of governments to find a solution to world problems. According to Hilsden, the question was: could such a state of affairs continue for much longer or would it all end relatively soon.

Horan attended the meting but did not speak. It was an Apostolic Ecclesia gig, but happened to promote beliefs that were almost identical to those that were causing Horan's trouble with the Catholic Church.

Horan never returned to the Apostolic Ecclesia group and left Hilsden's home soon after. His mission had by now become a one-man show. Living on welfare at his lodgings in Nunhead where he remains to this day, Horan continued to bombard journalists and media organisations with his writings.

The approaching millennium provided fodder for his most controversial prediction, that the world would end by the year 2000.

As the countdown to 2000 began and preparations for a worldwide party came to a head, Horan was predicting a completely different event.

One newspaper quoted Horan as advising the world's population not to 'bother making plans after the millennium because we're all going to die'.

'The most significant sign that the end of the world is near was the creation of the State of Israel which was foretold in the Bible. Israel's allies will be Britain, America, Canada, Australia and New Zealand. Saudia Arabia and many Commonwealth countries will also defend Israel,' he told the *Southwark News*.

When Horan was asked by the newspaper where he would be for the millennium, Horan replied he had nothing exotic planned, but was 'sure the Messiah will let me know'.

Horan also got in touch with world leaders from Saddam Hussein to the Dalai Lama to warn them about the imminent Armageddon.

In a letter addressed to 'Dear Rulers of the World', Horan asked Yasser Arafat, Ayatollah Rafsanjani and Colonel Ghadaffi for their response to 'a worldwide commonwealth of Israel', as well as recommending that they become 'adopted Jews'. And he went as far as to predict how an ultimatum from Jerusalem would read when the end of the world as we know it would arrive upon the second coming of Christ.

Addressed to all 'kings, queens, presidents, prime ministers, mayors, ambassadors and all political, military, academic and religious leaders, the ultimatum from Jesus Christ would demand that 'all nations who wish to continue their existence must become part of the worldwide commonwealth of Israel.'

The ultimatum would make three fundamental demands: 'That you and your people accept me as your king and immediately give up your position and office; that you accept the saints as your government, and that you accept all other conditions, especially that you accept the Jewish religion as your own.'

Horan claimed that the ultimatum would be unambiguous in its warning that a country's failure to meet these demands would lead to it being 'wiped off the face of the map'. Failure by an individual would mean that 'you will not be allowed to live any longer'.

The pamphlets and letters and Horan's behaviour didn't go unnoticed. In 1998, Horan met Dr Ulrike Schmidt, a consultant psychiatrist based at the Ivydale Mental Health Centre in London.

According to Dr Schmidt's medical report, Horan's appointment came about after Father Jeff Cridland and PC Terance O'Brien from Buckingham Palace's Intelligence Unit had tracked him down.

Horan had been sending numerous letters to a number of people at the Palace, which, although not 'threatening or offensive in nature, had been rather bizarre in content'. He had been telling senior figures inside Buckingham Palace that Princess Diana was an idol and God hated idols. Lady Di had been ousted for the Queen's sake, he claimed. At that point the Buckingham Palace Intelligence Unit decided that Horan needed help.

Dr Schmidt's report said Horan was, 'quite taken aback by the idea that anyone could be concerned about the pamphlets he had sent to members of the Royal family.'

Horan had accepted, she said, that many people felt his views were 'barmy', but stressed their importance and their non-threatening nature. He felt he had been victimised for having unusual religious beliefs, not least by the Catholic Church.

Dr Schmidt relayed Father Cridland's concerns that Horan had alienated many people and few were now having anything to do with him.

The banished priest was continuing to visit ex-parishioners on 'social calls', but these visits were also reaching their limit, according to Father Cridland.

In her assessment of his mental state, Dr Schmidt found Horan to be a middle-aged man who had good self-care. There was no evidence of any thought disorder, although she did remark that this might have become more evident had he discussed his beliefs.

'He described himself as low in mood in the mornings and also remarked that he had low energy until about midday. He said his sleep and appetite were fine. There was no evidence of any suicidal thoughts, he did express some hopelessness about life and the world in general...

'He seemed cognitively intact. He did not believe he was ill but acknowledged that others have seen him as ill.'

Dr Schmidt concluded there was longitudinal evidence that Horan suffered from a mild psychotic illness and that to some extent he responded to medication. She recommended he continue taking a mild dose of paroxetine, an anti-depressant drug.

As the millennium came and went, Horan continued to make use of every possible sporting or public event around London and the UK to dance his jig in his national costume in the hope that the world would take note of his message.

Holding a placard over his head while racing on to the running track at the Special Olympics World Games in Dublin in 2003 earned him a measure of publicity.

So did barging on to the centre court at Wimbledon the same year during a rain break in the Lindsay Davenport-Serena Williams clash. On that occasion, Horan slipped to his backside on the wet canvas, much to the amusement of the tennis fans, before police apprehended him and sent him home to Nunhead.

Consultations with psychiatrists petered out. He met them only when he was referred to them after some demonstration that drew police attention.

But the media was growing tired of the nutter priest. Horan felt his publicity campaign was fizzling out and needed a boost of worldwide proportions – a stunt the likes of which had never before been witnessed.

7

PRISONER JG 8046

Horan rose to his feet inside Northampton Magistrates Court. The courtroom was packed to capacity on 21 July 2003, mostly journalists sent to cover the outcome of one of the most bizarre sporting moments ever witnessed.

The Crown prosecution briefly outlined how the fifty-six-year-old Catholic priest ran on to Silverstone race track during the previous day's Grand Prix, narrowly escaping death and miraculously avoiding causing a serious or fatal accident. He had run along Hangar Straight in the opposite direction to Formula One cars racing at 200kmph, holding a placard over his head that said, 'Read the Bible, the Bible is Always Right'.

The magistrates retired for fifteen minutes before returning to give their verdict. 'I'm remanding Mr Horan in custody, to appear in court again in one week's time,' the chief magistrate said.

Horan was led away in a prison van. The previous day's lunatic stunt had landed the Kerry priest in jail for the first time. Inside Woodhill Category A Prison, Milton Keynes, Horan was given a number. For the next six weeks, he would no longer be known as Father Neil Horan. He was prisoner JG 8046.

The Grand Prix fiasco was the first dangerous stunt Horan had performed and stirred huge media interest across the world.

He claimed it all turned out quite differently from what he had originally planned – that an opportunity had arisen and he pounced on it.

One month earlier, in June 2003, Horan was entering Wimbledon underground station when he noticed a young woman giving out booklets. He took one and read it on the tube journey to Victoria. On page 33, the booklet listed sporting events scheduled for July and August that year, among them the British Grand Prix at Silverstone. Horan made up his mind there and then. He would take his publicity mission for the Bible to Formula One racing.

On the days before 20 July, Horan wrote out three cardboard posters, all with the words, 'Read the Bible, the Bible is Always Right'. On the morning of the final day of the Grand Prix, he packed his dancing costume in a case, together with his passport, his pre-purchased ticket to the race, a clock and an oil overcoat. He said goodbye to his landlady at 8am, telling her he was going to see a motor race.

He went by train from Nunhead to Victoria before taking the Circle Line tube to Euston and then travelled by taxi through the flat, green Northamptonshire countryside, arriving at a junction near Silverstone.

At the main gate to the circuit, Horan handed over his ticket and no questions were asked. Inside, he noticed the wire fencing all around, ranging from four to seven metres in height, with gates 100 metres apart. All the gates were either fully or partially closed, each one guarded by two stewards. Horan headed for the grandstand, thinking out the final elements of his plan:

'Even after arriving at the ground, I was not certain what exactly I was going to do. I felt that I could display the posters in front of the grandstand, either before the Grand Prix or during it. If that drew a bit of publicity for the Bible, I would have been satisfied. I had made up my mind to do this.

'I got a coffee and cake and sat down at a table, directly facing the track, which was no more than fifty metres away. Then a surprising sight met my eyes. There was a gate just opposite me, which was wide open, with no steward at it. I could scarcely believe my eyes that on such a day as this, there was an open gate, with no one guarding it.

'I took it as a sign from heaven. The gate was open for me. I thought I must go on to the track itself, to take the Bible to the world. My mind was made up in that instant.'

Horan glanced around and noticed a blonde steward about three metres away from the open gate. She was chatting to the spectators, as if one of them. Horan thought that if she was back at the gate by the time the Grand Prix started, he would have to force his way past her. Had this happened, he claims he would have stuck to his original plan of showing his placards in front of the grandstand.

'It soon came, the time when the public address system announced, "The Grand Prix will be starting in a few minutes." I waited to see the start and the first lap. Then I said to myself that it was time to go. I queued up for the toilet, which was in a caravan. There were five or six in front of me. There were only two toilets in the caravan. I knew I would be taking over one of them for a good while. I hoped that the others in the queue would not get impatient.

'Finally, I got in. The space was small enough. I put a small Bible into my shirt pocket, so that it was near my heart. As I began to change, I became aware, more than before, of the ferocious noise from the cars. It was simply deafening. When it came to tying my shoelaces, it must have taken me three minutes or more. Talk about shaking in your boots.

'I pulled on the raincoat, as I knew that the posters would draw unnecessary attention. If I had gone in front of the grandstand, that attention would have been all right, but not here. I opened the door and faced the world. As I climbed up the bank towards the gate, I thought I heard an 'aaahhhh' sound from the spectators nearby. I thought they had noticed me, they saw me in a raincoat on this hot July day.

'As I came within a few feet of the gate, cars were passing straight in front. I knew they would be around again in a few minutes. I sat down for perhaps a minute and a half. By now, there were two other stewards on the platform inside the gate. The steward with the blonde hair was still ten feet away. Everything was set. I could hear the cars approaching to my right. I said to myself, "This is it, this is the big one, it is time to make a move."'

With that, Horan slipped under the tape and walked quickly down the slope that led to the gate. He walked through the gate, a few feet from the two stewards. Within seconds, he was on the track. Horan began to change pace, breaking from a fast walk into a sprint.

'I was on the track. I thought briefly, "I am on the famous Grand Prix track at Silverstone." As I ran, I threw off my raincoat. I have never seen it since. The cars were on to me now. I felt myself drawn further and further on to the track. I could see cars, which were planning to overtake, swerve quickly back in line again, obviously at seeing me. Incredibly, I was hardly aware of the noise at all. Neither did I feel the slightest danger. All I can say is that God was with me.

'I kept running along the track. I looked up at a bridge which crosses the track at that place. There were twenty or more stewards on the bridge as I ran under the bridge. None of them seemed to make a move. All the bunch of cars had passed. I could see one last car coming, well behind the rest. I thought I would go really close to this now, since it was the last. I must have been within five feet of it.

'When it had passed, I kept running for a few seconds, then a steward grabbed me with a mighty rugby tackle. He said, "You should be dead." As he dragged me across the track, he squeezed my fingers something fierce. I thought he had broken them but fortunately he had not. He pulled me to the ground and held me down for a few seconds. Then one of his colleagues came and they both lifted me up over a wall, which was about five feet high, with a bank of grass at the top.

'As we reached the top, there were several spectators taking photos of me. A policeman appeared and the stewards handed me over to him. He led me through the crowd, down a slope, to a police van which was a short distance away from the racetrack and the spectators.'

The Formula One drivers that day could scarcely believe what appeared in front of them on the twelfth lap as they rounded the bend towards Hangar Straight, the fastest part of the circuit. Williams driver Juan Pablo Montoya immediately got on the car radio when he saw Horan on the track, prompting race officials to deploy the safety car. Jaguar's Antonia Pizzonia was one of the drivers who came closest to Horan, coming within feet of hitting the priest and miraculously avoiding an accident.

Afterwards, some of the drivers voiced their fury and recounted how lucky they were not to have mown down the mad priest or got themselves killed. British Formula One racing star, Jensen Button, was about to go left and overtake a car when he suddenly saw a 'madman on the track'. Button told reporters after the incident that he initially believed Horan was a girl because of the kilt. Button said: 'He endangered everyone's lives. It was very stupid. He obviously didn't care what happened to himself, but we care what happens to us.' Button finished eighth in the race – Brazilian Rubens Barrichello emerged victorious.

Button added: 'It was a very scary feeling and I was close enough to look into his eyes. He looked so weird and didn't seem to care if he was run over. He must have felt the wind from my car as I went by and is very fortunate no one hit him.'

Toyota's Cristiano da Matta said he was centimetres from hitting Horan, while Toyota team chief Eddie Jordan described the incident as 'shocking'.

Horan was delighted with the publicity but it was the last thing on earth Silverstone wanted or needed. The venue had already been subjected to a barrage of criticism by Formula One power-brokers Bernie Ecclestone and Max Mosley, and Horan's stunt raised further questions for the track's owners, the British Racing Drivers' Club. Ecclestone and Mosley had threatened to move the event to another country, possibly Turkey or India.

Before Horan was escorted from the circuit, the police drove him around in a van and asked him to point out where he had entered the track. As he waited to be questioned at Weston Favel Police Station, he chatted to police officers. Among them was an officer who told him she was a Christian who attended the Alpha Course, a series of religious talks organised jointly by Anglican, Catholic and other Churches.

'During the time I was in the cell in the police station, I had a lot of time to think. I came to the conclusion it was God who brought me to Silverstone that day. It was he who opened the gate for me. I was doing his work. He saved the drivers from accident and serious injury. I put the Bible on the world stage. It was the same Bible that protected me and the drivers from injury, with the help of God, of course.'

Two detectives, Julian Williams and John Austen, arrived to interview Horan. They questioned the prisoner at length about the day's events, before taking DNA and fingerprints and leading Horan back to his cell. By this time, the press was bombarding the police station with questions, trying to establish the identity of the nutter who had disrupted the race and forced the safety car to be deployed.

Police officers told Horan that he was being charged with aggravated trespass. He didn't sleep much that night and in the morning barely had enough time to have a light breakfast. Leaving the police station for court, he said goodbye to the officers and remarked to one, 'I should not be back here again'.

'Not unless you jump over something,' came the reply.

Horan was still wearing his dance costume because the suitcase carrying his ordinary clothes had not been returned – he had left it near the open gate at Silverstone. When he arrived at Northampton courthouse, Horan was given back his clothes, held a brief consultation with his lawyer, Paul Carter, and was taken to a holding cell to wait for his case to be called.

Handcuffed to two wardens, Horan was led up several flights of stairs and into the courtroom. The wardens chatted with the prisoner, remarking that they had been watching the race the previous day. After Horan was remanded in custody he was whisked away to Woodhill prison.

Prisoner JG8046 was put in a cell with Gary, a twenty-one year-old Irish traveller. From the age of fifteen, Gary had spent most of his life behind bars in a young offenders' unit. His wife had been banned from visiting him until October because she had insulted a warden. Horan's good friend, Father Hugh Bridge, wrote to the prison authorities, advising them of Horan's mental state. Based on this advice, Horan was moved to a cell on his own in the health wing where he would spend the following four weeks.

The reality of prison life began to hit Horan. 'It was like a different world, being locked in a small room, sometimes for twenty-two hours a day. Words could scarcely describe what it felt like. Oh, as I sat alone in my room, during those long days, how I longed to walk free down the street, go into a café for a cup of tea, open my own front door, sit at my desk, go on a bus, buy a newspaper, chat with a friend in the street, be uninterrupted in my room at night. All these things were denied to me now. There was the constant clanging of keys by the wardens, as they locked and unlocked doors. Your life is totally in the hands of other people. As Gary had said to me, "They more or less own you in here."'

Virtually every prisoner and warden inside Woodhill seemed to know who Horan was. Most had watched the race and several asked for Horan's autograph. Over the weeks, he became a figure of fun and ridicule, not alone in the newspapers, but inside the prison.

'Wherever I went, I would hear sounds of a certain motor race. One day, out in the exercise yard, I heard 'rrrrhhhh' coming from the direction of the gate. When I looked, it was two female wardens who were at it. I would hear, sometimes, in the distance, calls of 'pit stop', 'Silverstone Vicar', and 'Hanger Straight'. One warden remarked, 'You must be the most famous prisoner ever here.' Another told me how they were going change the name of Hanger Straight to 'Horan's Corner'. A good few of them said I shouldn't be here at all.'

While inside Woodhill, Horan wrote to the prison chaplain, offering to perform his Irish jig for prisoners and wardens. He was refused for 'security reasons', but renewed his offer as he left the prison on the day of his release.

He received several letters from friends, among them one from his landlady, Delia McManus. Over his six weeks inside, he befriended a number of inmates, including George Mullen, who was working in the prison toy shop. Mullen grew fond of Horan and continued to write to him for some time afterwards. This is a letter he sent to the priest weeks after Horan was released:

> Dear Neil,
> Well Neil mate I never thort you was going to write back but I'm ever so happy you did. It made my day you no speshley wen it come under my door and open'd it to find it was of you. Eney ways never guess wat I am doing. I work in the Noddy shop packen toys for the kids. Its ok but some times I get bord of it and so dus my brother. He is in this jail with me so I'm helping him out yeah like I shood be doing? Or yeah how you doing, I hope your keeping your self out of bother cos your to good for prison like if you no what I mean by that? Eney how I hope you stay in tuch with me mate cos I think highly of you as you're my good pal? Well Neil I'll end it for now so write back soon,
>
> God bless
> George

On 2 September 2003, Horan was brought to court again for sentencing. Wearing a grey tank-top and a white shirt, he sat impassively in the dock during the hearing. Prosecuting counsel Suraj Minocha told the court that Horan had pleaded guilty to aggravated trespass and outlined how he had previously carried out publicity stunts at Wimbledon and in front of the Houses of Parliament. Minocha told the court:

'During the police interview, Horan made it clear it was his intention to disrupt the race. The defendant is a man of strong religious beliefs who had little reaction from the press and politicians to previous actions...he told officers that he bought the ticket in advance but did not intend to enter the track until he saw an open security gate. He claimed it was a sign from God and changed his plan.'

Horan's solicitor, Paul Carter, told the court his client suffered from depression and what he had done was a 'substantial mistake but he did not see the consequences of his actions'. He assured the court that his client wouldn't appear before the magistrates again. 'It would be a mortal sin for him to kill himself or others. He has never hurt a person and will not do so in the future,' he said.

Probation officer Courtney Jones had interviewed Horan and read a psychiatric report written by consultant psychiatrist Dele Olajide. Jones told the court he believed, 'the possibility of him re-offending is very slim. He suffers from psychiatric problems including compulsive behaviour disorder and I would recommend a conditional discharge because I do not think this man will offend again.' The psychiatrist found him 'at all times a courteous and gentle soul who although possessed with a brilliant mind is nevertheless stuck in the concrete teachings of the Bible.' He wrote that while Horan had engaged in a reckless act, 'he is not a danger to the public and a non-custodial sentence is more likely to have a salutary effect on him.'

Horan was sentenced to two months but was freed. He had served six weeks in prison while on remand and was of good behaviour: 'For me, it was like a new birth, like starting life all over again. It was as if chains had been removed from my whole being, as if a heavy burden had been lifted from my shoulders. How I breathed the air of freedom, as we walked along, looking for a café. How I relished that first cup of tea as a son of freedom. The very cup, the spoon, the saucer, the table, they took on a new meaning, as if I should never again take anything for granted.

'Now, I had my life back again, a life that had been snatched from me on 21 July. How I felt, with a heavy heart, for all the prisoners I had left behind. How I longed that all of them could walk free that day with me.'

The vast majority of media commentators lambasted Horan for what he had done at Silverstone. The stunt was depicted as a lunatic act by a crazed man.

There were some exceptions, including one newspaper in his native County Kerry that had charted Horan's life for several years in keeping with the newspaper's policy of 'giving a voice to individuals or groups that find themselves in a distinct minority'. An editorial in *The Kingdom* written later that year called for support for Horan, going as far as to say he should be given a civic reception if he returned to Ireland:

'His decision to race on to the track at Silverstone while the British Grand Prix was in full flight was the act of a man desperate to get his point across and it confirmed that he was willing to risk his own life to be true to his convictions,' the article said.

And in a direct attack on the Catholic Church's response to the Bishop Eamon Casey scandal and to what had happened at Silverstone, the newspaper argued it was, 'interesting that senior officials in the Catholic Church, who were quick to appeal for respect for a bishop who fathered a child and used diocesan funds to hide the fact, are remaining strangely mute on the Father Neil Horan issue.'

But those who represented Horan or who supported him didn't know and weren't told the full story.

While inside the holding cell at the police station just hours after he wreaked havoc at Silverstone, Horan had already decided to pull off another crazed stunt.

He thought of how in the Gospels, Jesus laid a lot of stress in doing things in twos. He sent out his disciples two by two and 'where two or three are gathered together in my name, there I am in the middle of them.'

Like Jesus, Horan had also decided to do things in twos. He knew immediately after Silverstone that he would strike again. He had managed to fool them all.

8

SORRY VANDERLEI

British Airways Flight BA2640 from Gatwick to Athens on 28 August 2004 was delayed by one hour. Shortly after boarding, Horan fell asleep, relieved he had easily passed check-in and security.

Hardly a year out of prison after Silverstone, the Grand Prix priest was on his way to the Olympics to pull another publicity stunt. With no accommodation booked in Athens, the priest eventually found a waiting area near the arrivals lounge at Athens Airport where he could continue his rest for a few hours. It was almost dawn in Athens, several hours before Horan could make his way towards the location of the final leg of the Olympics marathon.

Police presence at the airport heightened Horan's fears. He worried he might be recognised from Silverstone. And he was aware that security at Athens was billed as being the tightest in the history of the Olympic games. For the first time, Horan was taking his publicity mission to a country and an event of which he had no experience. He was familiar with sporting events like the London Marathon, Wimbledon, major Derby races and even public Royal events in England, but Athens and the Olympics were a whole new ballgame.

By noon on Sunday, the temperature in Athens had risen to

above eighty degrees. Carrying a backpack, a large case and some hand luggage, Horan made his way to Panathinaikos Stadium, the home of the top Greek and European football side. When he arrived there, he was surprised to find the stadium locked, with no sign of activity anywhere in the vicinity. It seemed a most unlikely venue for the grand finish of the Olympic marathon.

Horan made his way to a nearby café and bought a cold drink. He was eventually put right in his mission by the man who served him. The man explained that the marathon was finishing at Panathinaiko Stadium, a venue several kilometres away and one often confused with the football grounds.

With the help of a street map, Horan made his way to Messogion Avenue, a long, wide thoroughfare in central Athens.

'It was so hot,' Horan recalls. 'I had five hours to pass, as the marathon was not scheduled to begin until 6pm. I lay down under some trees and fell asleep, terribly fearful of being robbed. What if my kilt or passport or money was taken?'

The afternoon drew on and the seemingly laid-back approach taken to spectator security for the race became clear to Horan. In the London Marathon, with which he was familiar, the majority of streets along the race route are protected by barriers erected the previous day and there is visible and extensive police and race steward presence.

But along Messogion, many of the barriers would not be erected until late afternoon on Sunday. There were no markings on the street and several gaps had been left in the barriers erected to separate the athletes from spectators.

Horan's greatest planning difficulty concerned where he would change into his costume comprising kilt, knee-high green socks, green underpants, green beret, black shoes and posters hanging back and front from his neck.

Moreover, the long white trenchcoat he planned to wear to conceal the costume hung to his ankles. Surely anybody wearing this coat in temperatures of almost 100 degrees would appear conspicuous, even mad. 'I remember drinking water from a tap because it was so hot. A Greek man but who had some English approached me and remarked how hot it was.

'I instantly grew paranoid. Was he a spy? Why did he approach me from the blue? My fears were really aroused.'

Horan knew the police were on alert for terrorists. It was not quite three years since the September 11 attacks in the United States. The cost of security for the Athens Olympics was budgeted at a staggering €1bn, three times as much as the Sydney Olympics, making it the most expensive policing operation in history.

He ventured into a public park, peeping through the bushes at the race route, hoping that the shrubbery would provide a temporary refuge to review his plan. He decided to move further down the race route. By 5pm, Horan was about three miles away from the marathon finish line.

He approached a café that had about twenty tables and seating outside, adjacent to the street and within yards of where the race was scheduled to pass. The only barrier between the spectators and the athletes was a length of tape stretched and tied about waist-high between the footpath and the street.

'The moment I saw the café I said to myself, "That's it! That's where I'll change." It was like divine inspiration.' Inside the café, Horan made his way to the toilet for the disabled. In less than an hour, the race leaders would pass and he grew more tense as he changed into his costume. And, as had happened in the toilet at Silverstone the previous year, his hands shook uncontrollably as he struggled to tie the laces on his black dancing shoes.

After twenty minutes he emerged from the toilet, his costume covered by the white trenchcoat. He bought a glass of fizzy orange, paid the waitress and took a seat outside the café.

Apart from a few raised eyebrows from a group of elderly women, Horan attracted no attention.

'About twenty minutes before the race leader passed, I knew that things were about to happen. Spectators began to stand up. I looked around me and noticed about twenty spectators in my vicinity. There was a steward about one hundred yards away and I knew it would be very easy to outwit him.

'Police cars passed at high speed, one about every five minutes. How could they have spotted me travelling at that high speed?

'I had left the big poster in the case and had just one poster on my front and one on the back.

'Then I saw a police car approaching. Behind it was a truck. I couldn't see behind it, but by the time it passed, the crowd was cheering.

'The minute the lorry passed, there he was. He was no more than ten feet away from the lorry. He was so small, like a schoolboy, probably Ethiopian.

'I wondered if he was a decoy. Then I realised he was the race leader. There were no ifs or buts about it.'

Thirty-five-year-old Brazilian marathoner Vanderlei de Lima was a surprise leader for the fans and the media.

The five-foot, five-inches runner from Cruzeiro de Oeste worked on peasant farms before he became a professional athlete. Despite having won the bi-championship in the Pan-American Games and achieving good results in Japan and Europe, he was relatively unknown. Until now.

Horan made an instant decision to pounce. He flung off his

trenchcoat, ducked under the tape and made a dash, sprinting as fast as he could to get ahead of de Lima.

He rushed at a right angle directly towards de Lima, flinging his hands around him, two fingers of his left hand clutching the athlete's singlet. The two men veered off the street towards the footpath before crashing to the ground.

The gasp of surprise from the spectators quickly turned to anger. For about three to four seconds, spectators looked on in astonishment, stunned by what they were witnessing. All but one spectator, local man Polyvios Kossivas.

Kossivas had been watching the marathon in the comfort of his own home just a short distance away. Intrigued by de Lima's performance, he made his way to where Horan launched his attack to watch the race.

Now a salesman and hailed a hero in Brazil, Kossivas was the only spectator to come to the aid of de Lima. He jumped over the tape barrier and threw himself on top of the priest. He subdued Horan and helped de Lima back on his feet, steering him back on to the race route and shouting, 'Go, go!' According to Kossivas, de Lima lost about twenty-one seconds.

'It was visible that his [de Lima's] heart was stomping, completely upset by what had just happened,' Kossivas told journalists afterwards.

De Lima surged on, shaking his head in disbelief. By the time he reached Panathinaiko Stadium, Stefano Baldini from Italy had passed him to win the gold medal, as well as American Meb Keflezighi to win the silver.

It was de Lima who got the hero's welcome. As he rounded the final bend and headed for the finish line, the stadium erupted. In an astonishing display of Olympic spirit, de Lima smiled and imitated an aeroplane as he completed the final hundred metres to cross the finish line. In de Lima's own words afterwards, 'Olympic spirit prevailed.'

'My determination prevailed again,' he said. 'I was able to medal for myself and medal for my country.'

De Lima believed he could have won gold were it not for Horan's crazed stunt. 'For the way I was running, I was unstoppable. I had some troubles in the first kilometres, but I was in great shape and I'm sure I would have won it. The attack really surprised me, because I did not think I was his target. He did not injure me, but he broke my rhythm and I lost concentration. I didn't know if he had a weapon or what his intention was.'

Most experts agreed de Lima's lead was shrinking even before Horan struck and a silver medal was the most likely result. The view is bolstered by the little-reported fact of the carbohydrate gel that came strapped to de Lima's bottle at the previous water station. The gel takes about ten minutes to take effect and it was the athlete's last sustenance before the finish line.

Despite an appeal by de Lima and the Brazilian Olympic Council (BOC), the International Association of Athletics Federations (IAAF) ruled that the race result would stand.

There was some consolation, however, when de Lima was awarded the Pierre de Coubertin medal at the closing ceremony by the International Olympic Committee 'in recognition of de Lima's exceptional demonstration of fair play and Olympic values'.

In his home country, de Lima was hailed a hero and voted Brazilian personality of the year.

Horan claims if de Lima was physically bigger, the stunt would not have ended as it did.

'I said sorry to de Lima after we fell to the ground and I told him that I did not mean it to come to this.

'When it happened, the spectators shouted at the top of their voices. I heard one Italian shouting, "What are you doing? You're a devil, you're Satan. You've ruined this man's chances."

'I remember a policeman with glasses grabbed me by the shoulders and picked me up. The crowd tried to grab my ankles and pull my hair. Another police officer then came to my side and the two policemen walked me to a police car about fifty yards away.'

Within hours of being arrested and taken to a station of the General Police Division of Attica, Horan received a phone call from an official at the Irish Embassy in Athens.

Despite the language barrier, Horan knew by the demeanour of the police officers that many of them were angered by what had happened. After all, he had shown them up in front of the world. However, he describes the treatment he received from the Greek police as reasonable and fair, except for two separate incidents he found most unusual.

Shortly after his arrest, Horan and one officer were left alone in a room. 'I felt this man had a threatening manner. He went to the press and took out a piece of wood. There were more instruments, like cricket bats, inside the cupboard. He began to wield it at me and was saying something in Greek. He then came over and put the end of it against my stomach. I put my hands in the air and said, "Oh no." Finally, he put it back in the press and some more officers came in. It was the only threat or violence used against me while I was in police custody.'

The second incident occurred later that evening when Horan claims he was left alone in a room in the police station.

For a few minutes he listened to loud laughter coming from the adjacent room before one officer entered. He spoke relatively good English.

'This officer said, "I want to make a proposal to you". He then told me that Parathinaikos were to play Arsenal in a football match some time later, I can't recall. He then said, "We want you to run on to the pitch to stop the match and we will bet on you." He said he was a member of Interpol and he would ensure that I was bailed out. He seemed serious.

'I told him certainly not. I thought it an extraordinary thing for a member of a police force to do. I knew he was serious afterwards because I remember hearing or seeing something about the match he spoke about.'

Horan spent the night in the station cell and was taken by police escort to a scheduled court sitting early on Monday morning. Outside the courthouse, a large press corps had gathered, excited about getting a shot of the nutty priest who had wreaked havoc the previous day.

Two embassy officials accompanied Horan inside the court building. But legal representation posed a problem. A lawyer approached Horan and demanded a fee of €250. Horan told him and the embassy officials he didn't have enough money with him and that accessing money would prove very difficult.

The embassy officials made contact with Dan Horan, Neil's brother. 'When I spoke to Dan, he said to me, "What about Medugorje now?" I had planned to go to Medugorje that week but Dan felt that this was now in doubt. 'I remember asking Dan if what I did was in the news. He totally misinterpreted my question. I wanted to know that so I could realise what my family knew and didn't know. Dan felt I wanted to know for the glory.

'He then told me he couldn't send me the money until about 11.30am Athens time, which was 9.30am at home in Ireland. It turned out that it wasn't good enough for the lawyer so I decided to represent myself in court.'

At home in County Kerry, Dan Horan had been inundated with calls from journalists, friends and family members from late Sunday night. Television footage of his brother's latest stunt had been beamed across the world. The events in Athens angered Dan Horan and he was not shy in expressing his feelings to journalists.

In one interview, he called on his brother to 'Stop the madness', and commented that a few years in jail would do his troublesome sibling the world of good. He also subsequently said he believed Neil needed proper and continuous psychiatric assessment and treatment.

The Athens fiasco was causing a split in the Horan family. Neil's actions hurt and embarrassed Dan and the others. Dan Horan's comments hurt and embarrassed Neil.

Back in Athens, Horan sat on a bench at the back of the courtroom, flanked by two police officers. The younger of the two officers reassured him, telling him that he was a good man and they were not worried about his destiny.

Horan's case was called. He moved to the front of the courtroom and stood before the three judges, accompanied by a translator.

'The charge was read out to me. All I can recall is that it had something to do with interfering with an athlete and disrupting a race.

'I was asked if I had anything to say and I said, "Yes." I apologised for not having a lawyer but explained that I did not have €250 and was representing myself. The presiding judge questioned me about my name and I knew they found Cornelius difficult to pronounce. He asked me had I ever been in court before and I told him about the Silverstone Grand Prix.'

The Greek legislation that covered Horan's actions was

different from the law that applied in the UK when he caused chaos at Silverstone. On that occasion, he was convicted of aggravated trespass. In Athens, he had violated Greek laws pertaining to extracurricular sports.

Displaying numerous press cuttings he had brought with him to Athens, Horan again addressed the judge, apologising to the Olympic Committee, to Vanderlei de Lima and to the Greek people.

'The judge then said, "The court finds you guilty." He said, "I sentence you to twelve months in prison and fine you €3000." My heart sank.

'Then he resumed, saying he would suspend the sentence on condition that I not come back to Greece and disrupt any event in Greek life. He also banned me from watching the Olympic games. I thanked the judge and bid farewell to the land of Greece. I also vowed never again to disrupt any event.'

As Horan left the court, accompanied by two police officers, reporters hurled questions at him from the court steps. But he was quickly bundled into a police car and driven to a police station near Athens Airport to meet British Airways security personnel. After one more night in police custody in Athens, Horan was accompanied by two British Airways security officers on a flight to Heathrow.

On the flight, television news pictures showed footage of the extraordinary events at the marathon in Athens. Horan missed the clip as he had fallen asleep.

By the time he arrived home to Nunhead, de Lima and the Brazilian Olympic Council were appealing the outcome of the marathon. Through the media Dan Horan was appealing to his brother to stop his madness and a media frenzy was in full swing in Greece, Brazil, Ireland and the UK.

Horan vowed to travel to Brazil to apologise personally to de Lima and the Brazilian people. But bail conditions relating to another pending court case restricted his travel. Instead, Horan wrote a letter to the Brazilian athlete, apologising for what had happened and swearing, 'by Almighty God that I never intended going anything like as far as I did'. He also offered to travel to Brazil to do his peace dance. Horan has never received a response.

Carlos Artur Nuzman, President of the Brazilian Olympic Committee, criticised race organisers for what had happened. He accepted that what had happened de Lima ought to be called 'an accident', but stressed there were 'serious security lapses'.

It was undeniable, he said, that the incident altered the race result.

Ironically, finishing third rather than first turned out almost better for de Lima. Dozens of camera crews were at São Paulo airport to greet the hero home. During his first television interview, one of the Brazilian beach-volleyball gold medallists took off his medal and placed it around de Lima's neck.

Brazil's largest supermarket chain, Pão de Açúcar, gave him the 200,000 Brazilian reais (€88,000) promised to all gold medal winners, not the 70,000 reais pledged to bronze medallists. de Lima joined Ronaldo, Roberto Carlos and the Brazilian football squad at a training session on the eve of a World Cup qualifier. Days later, he met with Brazilian President Luiz Inácio Lula de Silva before the annual Independence Day parade in Brasilia.

De Lima quickly became king of the TV and radio chat-show circuit and his agent, Jos Hermens, estimated that de Lima's appearance fee grew tenfold to €200,000 immediately after his clash with Horan in Athens.

Kossivas, too, basked in the media attention. The Brazilian

Olympic Committee flew him to Rio de Janeiro, where he was given VIP treatment for the duration of his stay and dubbed 'the Greek angel'. He walked on to the pitch at the Maracana Stadium before a Brazilian football game and was taken as a guest of honour to watch an Ayrton Senna motor racing exhibition in São Paulo. At the Brazilian Athlete of the Year prizegiving ceremony, Kossivas was called on the stage and he and de Lima emotionally embraced. It was the first time the two had met since Athens.

The crème-de-la-crème of Brazilian sport gave the two a standing ovation and Kossivas returned home with a jade trophy mounted on a granite pedestal, a special gift given to him by de Lima on behalf of the BOC.

Horan had fulfilled his intention to carry out the second part of the 'double witness', where many things in the Bible are done in twos.

In the days that followed the Athens chaos, journalists scoured thesauruses to find new adjectives to describe Horan. Words like 'nutter', 'crazed', 'madhatter' and 'lunatic' all featured in newspaper copy.

Horan publicly vowed never to break the law again, repeatedly claiming that he had never intended to go as far as he did or to harm de Lima. The following year he higlighted the reason he targeted sporting events in an interview with Swiss journalist Stepheney Shaerar.

Horan claimed that sport gets far too much media attention and occupies a place in the public mind which ought to be devoted to the Bible and debate around the 'purpose of life on earth'. He objected to 'making sport into a business and treating it as if it were crucial for all of us'.

He targeted Silverstone and Athens, he said, 'to point out to the sporting world that there are more important things than sport', and to tell the world that people have 'exalted sport far too high'.

On numerous occasions after Silverstone, Horan was subjected to ridicule on the street, in the shops and on public transport. To most people, the episode appeared crazy but because nobody was injured, they were prepared to look on it as funny.

Athens was different. For the first time, Horan's publicity stunt had an identifiable victim. Somebody had borne the brunt of his crazed actions –Vanderlei de Lima.

As Horan took part in the St Patrick's Day parade in London the following year, some choice remarks were hurled at him. One young man shouted: 'You're a right bollocks after what you did to that young fellow in the Olympics.'

On another occasion, as Horan performed his peace jig at Leicester, he had a conversation with a boy no more than nine or ten years old. The boy asked, 'Are you the Grand Prix priest?'

'Yes.'

'You're a dickhead. You're winded now after a few minutes dancing. How do you think that runner felt in the Olympics after two hours? Why did you do that to him?'

'I did it for the Bible and for Christ.'

'You did to for yourself. You're on an ego trip.'

Many people believed that the de Lima episode Athens would be the last the world saw of Horan. But they were wrong again. In the background lurked much more, something totally unrelated and far more sinister.

9

THE TRIAL

Horan took a seat in the dock in Court 17 at the Old Bailey on the morning of 25 October 2004. Wearing black carpet slippers and a black patterned jumper, he massaged a set of rosary beads as he listened to Frank McGrath tell the jury of seven women and five men that the Crown prosecution would prove the priest guilty of gross indecency with a child.

McGrath told the court that on a date unknown in the early 1990s, while he wasa practising priest, a lady friend and her young daughter visited Horan at his residence. During the course of that visit, Horan lay down naked on a bed with the girl and her mother passionately tickling him.

Horan's most serious brush with the law had ignited eight months earlier. It was 7.10am on 1 March when the front doorbell rang at 25 Howbury Road in London. Delia McManus, Horan's landlady, pulled on her dressing gown and went to open the door.

Outside stood police constables Sam Renwick-Forster and Claire Moulinie, along with Detective Kevin Colville. They asked to see Father Neil Horan and Delia McManus went to get him.

In the sitting room of the house the police told Horan that a young woman had accused him of gross indecency during the time he was a priest in Anerley parish. The incident was alleged to have happened about thirteen years earlier when the woman was seven or eight years old. After a twenty-minute conversation with the police, Horan was arrested and cautioned, to which he replied: 'Yes, I was naked.'

Horan dressed himself and was taken in a police van to Peckham police station. He was released on bail to return to the station three weeks later. On that occasion police conducted a taped interview with him, in which he admitted that he had been naked in front of the child. He was charged with gross indecency.

By this time, dealings with the British police and the law were no longer strange to Horan. He had been arrested and jailed over Silverstone and was relatively familiar with court procedure. However, Horan was stunned by the allegation of gross indecency. He couldn't believe that an incident that had happened years previously was the subject of a criminal investigation. What he faced was far more serious than anything that had happened before.

When the police officers made the allegation, Horan knew the young girl to whom they referred. He also knew her mother very well. Both mother and daughter were parishioners he had befriended while in Anerley, and the alleged incident related to an afternoon the two of them came to visit Horan at his home.

On 23 January, five weeks before Horan was arrested, the mother had written to Father Barry Hughes, Horan's predecessor at Anerley. In the letter, she accused Horan of indecent exposure while she and her daughter visited Horan's house to watch a 'Wild History' video.

In the letter, the mother alleged that Horan had removed his underpants and 'ran around starkers in an enlarged state playing hide and seek with [her daughter]'.

She claimed her daughter had informed her that she 'touched' Horan. Her daughter, she said, was unable to move on and was still quite upset about what had happened.

The letter explained that the woman had tried to remain friends with Horan over the years but her reluctance to act on the allegations had made her daughter feel she didn't care about what had happened. The mother also alleged that Horan had remarked, on another occasion, that, 'young children can be very attractive'.

She claimed in the letter that Horan had quoted sexual references from the Bible. She believed it was wrong for a person to, 'go around nude in front of children, or adults for that matter,' and, 'the fact he is a priest makes it much worse'.

The mother concluded her letter to Father Hughes by saying that she could not live with herself if she did not report the allegation and that she was sorry she hadn't reported the matter sooner.

Father Hughes immediately relayed the allegations made by the mother to the relevant Church authorities and they made their way to the police. On foot of the allegations, the police arrested and charged Horan.

Two weeks after she wrote to Father Hughes, the mother told police in a written statement that she had remarked to Horan in the room on the day of the alleged incident: 'You might as well not wear them [underpants]; you leave nothing to the imagination'. At this point, she claimed, Horan removed his underpants and began to chase her daughter around the room.

She said she did not go into all the detail of what had happened that day in the letter she wrote to Father Hughes because, 'It is a respect thing and it would be terribly embarrassing'.

In her statement to police on 13 February 2004, the young

woman at the centre of the allegation claimed that she had been seven or eight years old at the time. She said she recalled going to Horan's living accommodation attached to St Anthony's Church and being in a big room upstairs which had a bed and TV.

The incident I referred to happened only once when I was in Father Horan's room with my mum present. My mum took me to his room. I remember being in his room and that Father Horan was wearing only green underpants.

The next thing I remember is Father Horan laying down naked on the floor with an erect penis. I went over to him and began touching his erect penis. I was pushing and pulling it a few times. Father Horan was laughing.

At the time I didn't know what was happening and thought it was a game. The next thing I remember is Father Horan sitting on a chair and was about to sit me on his lap. He was still naked. My mum told him to put his pants on before he sits me on his lap. Father Horan put his pants on and then sat me on his lap.

I can't remember how it stopped. I do remember visiting Father Horan's room on other occasions either before or after this incident.

Since he moved parishes to Nunhead I have visited him there with my mother and nothing ever happened. I have also seen him since when he has come to my mother's for dinner.

I have never mentioned the incident to him. My mother has written to complain only after constant arguments between mum and me. This is because I would always bring the matter up in arguments.

I want this man punished for what he did to me. I now know this was not a game but something wrong and indecent.

From the outset, Horan admitted that he was naked on the day in question. But at all times he denied that he allowed the daughter to touch him and denied being guilty of gross indecency.

On 13 April, Horan formally entered a not-guilty plea in court. But the district judge at Greenwich Magistrates' Court took the view that the accusation made against Horan was too serious to be heard by the Magistrates' Court and declined jurisdiction. This meant that Horan would be sent forward for trial before a jury at the Old Bailey.

As the trial approached, Horan's legal team warned him on a number of occasions not to have any contact with the Crown Prosecution Services or with the officers involved in the case. In one letter, his solicitor warned him that he could be 'undermining' his case if made any further contact.

The warning came after Horan insisted to his legal team that he give his side of the story before the case ever went to trial.

In a lengthy statement addressed to Detective Kevin Colville and to Child Protection Agency officers, Horan said he prayed that God would strike him dumb if what he was about to write was not the truth.

He explained that he first came to know the mother and her daughter after Sunday Mass one morning in Anerley in September 1990. He grew to be good friends with the mother, often having dinner with her.

A single mother at the time, she was interested in converting to Catholicism.

Horan was moved to Nunhead in 1992 and his friendship with the mother continued and intensified: 'On several occasions, if the weather was fine, we went to Peckham Rye Park. [The mother] would ask me: "Can I hold your hand?" I agreed, with the greatest reluctance. She insisted, no matter how much I explained to her that this is just not normal practice with a Catholic priest. In all my years as a priest, no other woman ever made that request of me...'

Horan told officers that the mother then wanted to him to celebrate her daughter's First Holy Communion Mass, rather than the parish priest, Father Cridland. He claimed that rumours about their relationship began to circulate in the parish.

'There were all kind of rumours of us being lovers. Some even suggested I might be [the daughter's] father. The rumours got so serious that the subject was brought up at a meeting of one of the parish committees.

'One Monday morning, I met [a parishioner] in the kitchen. She was crying. I asked what the matter was and she said: [Another parishioner] said to me yesterday Father Neil and [the mother] are having sex upstairs while [the daughter] is down here...

'We used to stroll around Penge and through Crystal Palace Park. An odd time [the daughter] would be between us as we each held her by a hand..

'I spent six weeks in Woodhill Prison, Milton Keynes. While I was there, I received seven letters from one particular lady. I have them all here. They are warm and uplifting, with many quotations from the Bible. It must have taken ages to write them. Who is that lady? [The mother]...

Horan's letter to the police and the Child Protection Agency argued that 'one swallow didn't make a summer' and that he should not be judged on one act.

It was just that once, he said, that he went 'naked in front of females' and both mother and daughter were in the best positions to judge his character.

'Apart from that one act, can they cast another single thing against me? Have I told dirty jokes to them? Have I uttered one improper, lewd or unwholesome word? Have I made one untoward sexual suggestion? Have I told lies? Have I lived up to my word? Has my conversation ever been trivial or degrading? Have I made a single improper gesture with my body?

'I showed [the mother] several videos. Were any of these improper? If they have anything to cast against me here, I dare them to come forward with it.'

The mother in the case had explained away the thirteen-year gap between the time of the alleged incident and it being reported to the authorities by her wish to continue her friendship with Horan.

In his letter, Horan claimed he was accused of indecency only after he tried to cool off his relationship with the mother:

'The last time I visited [the mother] was in November (2003). I always told Delia, my landlady, when I was going to [the mother's] place. This was so Delia would not cook me dinner as I would have it with [the mother]. I always returned after midnight.

'Delia said to me: "Be careful or else people will start talking like they did before. The papers said you are a deeply religious person, now live up to it. Remember you're a priest."

'Delia is well aware of the talk that was going around Nunhead parish ten years ago. I made up my mind, there and then, that I would have to distance myself from [the mother].

'I said nothing to her that evening. I decided to wait until Christmas, which was only a short time away. Then I intended to tell her that, in the New Year, my visits would be far fewer, at most every three months.

'She had to cancel my next visit, as she was sick. I have not been over to see her since. I could have easily have picked up the phone, at any time and asked at least how she was. I could have written a letter. I could have sent a Christmas card. I did none of these things, deliberately so.

'I am sure she felt snubbed by me… hell hath no fury like a woman scorned.'

Frank McGrath, for the prosecution, said the Crown would prove that Horan lay down naked on his back while the mother and her daughter were visiting.

He told the jury that Horan denied any act of gross indecency and had written to the police, admitting he had taken off his shorts and was 'lying on the bed with the girl and her mother passionately tickling me'.

In her evidence in court, the daughter stuck to her statement, claiming that Horan had allowed her touch his penis and rub it for ten seconds or more.

The girl's mother was adamant in her evidence in court that Horan had become sexually aroused. But she said at no time had she seen her daughter's hand on his penis or fondling it, despite admitting she was fairly close to them at all times.

She told the court that she had remained good friends with Horan over the years, including the previous year when he was jailed for running on to the racing circuit at the British Grand Prix.

Julia Krish for the defence cross-examined the mother. She

put it to her: 'You were there for him on his release (from prison) and you have been there for him ever since?'

'Yes,' the mother replied.

Ms Krish put it to the witness that Horan believed it perfectly natural to be naked.

'Yes,' replied the witness.

The mother then told the jury Horan may have taken off his vest and pants because he misunderstood her sarcastic remark, 'You might as well take them all off.'

By the time Horan took the witness box to give evidence, the mother and daughter were no longer in the courtroom to hear what he had to say.

Horan explained that he had enjoyed a very close relationship with the woman and her daughter and that the mother had visited him twenty times before.

'Of all the thousands of women I have met, there was a different relationship with her from any other. It was the closest and most intense I have ever had with a woman,' he told the court.

But he insisted the relationship was platonic and denied that he ever had sexual intercourse with the mother or with any other woman.

He would remain celibate, he said, 'until my dying day'.

Horan told the jury that on the day in question, thirteen years previously, he had just had a bath. He was wearing his green underpants and had rubbed cream on his legs because he was suffering from a persistent itch.

'The only green underpants I wear are these ones,' he recalled. They are the ones I have always worn for Irish dancing. They have to be kept in good shape. They are the ones I wore in Athens.'

Horan produced the green underpants in the witness box,

explaining that these were the ones he always wore when performing his peace jig.

Members of the jury laughed when trial Judge Gerald Clifton asked, 'Do you wear something on top of them?'

'My kilt,' replied Horan. 'I'm not just saying I wear them.'

The witness went on to explain how on the day in question, 'The moment the mother saw me she said, "Can you put some clothes on, please?"

'I explained to her that I had put some cream on and it was not drying and would it be okay if I just wore what I was wearing. She said okay.'

Horan told the court he and the mother talked and then the mother suggested he take off his pants.

'The next thing I remember was the mother saying: "You might as well take everything off now," and I did.

'As I think about it now and I look back, I did not take it as sarcasm. I took it then as a serious request.

'We could all speculate as to why she said those words. I took them as literal and serious. If people are joking, I tend to take them seriously.

'I remember being absolutely amazed at the lack of reaction and surprise she showed.

'It was all as natural as grass growing in a field. Strange as it may seem, we went on as if I was wearing clothes.

'The next thing I remember was a game of hide and seek. We had played it many times in the mother's flat.'

Horan told the court he lay on the bed because his back began to hurt. He said the mother and daughter began to tickle him on the left side of his ribs. 'The mother has always gone in for a lot of tickling. She seems to make a habit of it, therefore even at that stage it didn't surprise me that much,' he told the jury.

At that point, Julia Krish for the defence directly asked Horan if he had allowed indecency to take place.

Horan looked at the jury, raised his arms to the heavens and intoned: 'Everyone here present, I call on you to witness at this moment. I call on Almighty God in heaven to strike me dead if I did such a thing.'

He told the court that the allegation that he had allowed the girl to touch him was 'an abominable lie'.

'I didn't allow her touch my penis. If that had taken place I would fell physically sick. I would feel like vomiting. It is absolutely false and it didn't happen. I am sticking to the truth and nothing more or nothing less than the truth.'

He would never harm a child, he said, as those who do are 'cast into the sea' in the Bible.

At one point during his evidence, Horan broke down, burying his face in his hands and weeping uncontrollably. The court adjourned for a brief period while he composed himself, before Horan returned to the witness box, wiping his eyes with a handkerchief.

Father Hugh Bridge had known Horan on and off for twenty-five years and worked in a neighbouring south-east London parish. In his evidence, he told the court that Horan had changed since he first came to know him as a curate.

When asked by Julia Krish for his opinion of Horan, Father Bridge replied: 'To be honest, a bit of a nutcase. He has got very strong views of an Aryanist nature about the second coming of Christ that have placed him at odds with the ecclesiastical authorities.'

Some of Horan's views, Father Bridge testified, could be attributed to mental illness. However, he said Horan's religious views were, at all times, sincerely held.

In his summary to the jury, Judge Gerald Clifton said the girl's mother had insisted that Horan was sexually aroused. But at no time, he said, did the mother see her daughter's hand touching Horan's penis, despite being just feet away in the same room.

The Judge reminded the jury that Horan had said in his evidence: 'That part of my body is extremely sensitive. Had I had an erection, I would have known about it. I never had, nor never will I have, sex with a woman'.

Judge Clifton also commented that a number of character witnesses had given evidence on Horan's behalf, including Horan's eighty-five-year-old landlady, Delia McManus. She and other character witnesses had attested to Horan's trustworthiness and their belief that the accused was incapable of committing the offence. He reminded the jury that one of the character witnesses, Father Hugh Bridge, had described Horan as 'a bit of a nutcase'.

At the end of the three-day trial, the jury at the Old Bailey retired to deliberate on the evidence. The case had eventually come down to a conflict of evidence: it was Horan's word against that of the mother and her daughter.

In less than an hour, the jury returned and informed the court it had reached a unanimous verdict on the two counts of indecency. Horan rose to his feet as the verdict was read aloud: the priest was found not guilty.

Horan looked emotional and relieved. He hugged his barrister Julia Krish, then left the courtroom to change into his red kilt, emerald green vest, socks and beret – as well as the green satin underpants he had displayed in court.

Outside the courtroom, Horan danced a celebratory jig. Speaking to reporters, he thanked his supporters and – now that he was free to do so – vowed to travel to Brazil as soon as possible to apologise personally to Vanderlei de Lima, the Brazilian athlete he had infamously tackled to the ground in Athens just months before.

As he spoke to reporters, Horan covered his eyes and choked back tears. He warned that his experience should serve as a lesson for other priests that apparently innocent behaviour could be misconstrued: 'It is a warning to celibate priests that they have to take great care with female members of their congregations. Celibate priests are extremely vulnerable when dealing with unmarried mothers, single women, divorced women and so on.'

Horan went home to Howbury Road, physically and emotionally exhausted after his court ordeal. That night, the phone rang and Horan answered. It was the girl's mother, ringing to congratulate him on the verdict which had been relayed to her and her daughter by the police.

Those close to Horan believed that allegations made against him and his Old Bailey trial would surely end his relationship with the mother. They were wrong. Two days after the end of the trial, a six-page handwritten letter arrived at Horan's home. He opened it, immediately recognising the handwriting. It was from the mother, penned the day after his trial ended.

The letter was a grovelling apology for what had happened, full of guilt. It explained to Horan the series of events that led to him standing trial.

The mother wrote that she had gone to the police on the advice of Canon John Kavanagh, the Child Protection Coordinator in the Southwark Diocese. 'Although I did go, when told, to the police, I didn't contact them in the first place. There was no time to actually consider if I actually wanted the police involved. I do admit I wrote to Father Barry (Hughes) and I wish I hadn't.

'It seemed only a matter of time before something happened

because (my daughter) was telling people she touched you, which of course, I did not see.'

The mother told Horan that shortly before the case was to go to trial, she 'broke down, realising it was my stupid remark that had caused this. I left a message on your phone and wrote to you and Father Kavanagh, asking him to pass on to Hither Green (police) that I wanted out. I went to Penge Police Station to drop the charges, as promised, but was told there were no officers available…

'If I did not go to court, I would be arrested for contempt of court and could go to prison.

'The same officer came to see me the Sunday before and issued me with a summons which I had to sign for Woolwich Crown Court. If I tried to run away, someone would come and get me and take me to court…

'I sincerely did not realise how much the fault was mine and I am very sorry.

'[My daughter's] name cannot be mentioned, nor mine, in case she becomes known by people seeing me. I would think everyone knows already.

'I admit to saying, "Why don't you take everything off?" I admitted this to the police. They said it wasn't my fault. I told them I felt it was my fault. I will admit it to whoever they may be.'

She feared that although Horan had been cleared of the charges, her remarks on the day in question and Horan's subsequent actions might lead to him being stripped of his collar and defrocked.

She finished her letter: 'Although I have hurt you, that was not my intention. I don't expect forgiveness from you or anyone else. I don't deserve your friendship, nor do I deserve anyone else's friendship. I enclose a stamped addressed envelope. Could you just say if the letter arrived? Thank you. God bless and keep you safe from all harm…'

Despite all that had happened, the friendship did not end. Horan and the mother continued to correspond, exchanging cards and letters.

Just months later, Horan would find himself in yet another crisis. Among the band of supporters to rally round in his hour of need would be the woman who gave sworn evidence against him in front of judge and jury at the Old Bailey.

10

KICKED OUT FOR GOOD

The two-page Vatican decree pulled no punches:

> Supreme Pontiff, Pope John Paul II, having heard the
> merits of the case concerning the above named priest
> of the Archdiocese of Southwark, and after careful
> consideration, by a supreme decision against which
> no appeal is possible, decrees that the said priest
> (Cornelius Horan) is hereby dismissed.

The decree was signed by Cardinal Josef Ratzinger, Prefect of the Congregation for the Doctrine of the Faith and Pope-to-be.

But it was Pope John Paul II, once photographed warmly embracing the Kerry cleric in Rome, who officially kicked Horan out of the priesthood for good.

Horan suspected that the request to attend the house of the Archbishop of Southwark, Kevin McDonald, had something to do with his future in the Catholic Church. Monsignor Richard Moth's letter requesting the meeting didn't give any details. It merely told Horan that the Archbishop wished to meet him at the suggested time of 5pm on 20 January 2005.

In the wake of Silverstone, Athens and a three-day court trial for gross indecency involving a child, Horan rightly reckoned he wasn't calling round for a theological discussion over afternoon tea. In fact, days before the meeting, Horan second-guessed his superiors in an effort to garner public support and weaken the Church's hand. He contacted a number of journalists about the meeting, claiming that he believed he was about to be stripped of his collar without good or proper reason.

When Horan arrived outside the Archbishop's house he met a number of reporters there. He spoke to them briefly, outlining the importance of the Bible. Then he danced in full costume – brown kilt, green waistcoat and matching beret – 'to bring a little joy to the occasion'. Inside, Monsignor Moth and Archbishop McDonald sat across a desk from Horan. They had a number of documents to hand. Horan was armed too, his most powerful weapon a copy of his book *A Glorious New World*.

He expected a trial of sorts, one similar in procedure to his experience at the Old Bailey just months earlier. But his Church superiors had a different idea: 'Imagine my shock, when I went in and found that there was no hearing at all, but a presentation of a fact to me, the fact that I had been put out without even the semblance of the due process which the Church's own laws lay down. Archbishop Kevin handed me a letter, which turned out to be the decree laicising me. He briefly explained what it was, then presented me with another letter, which he asked me to sign. This letter was very brief, and just stated that I had accepted the decree. I said, "I am signing nothing."

'Not only were they presenting me with a letter of dismissal from Rome but asking me to sign that I meekly accepted it. I had no intention of doing any such thing.

'The Archbishop then handed me a third letter, which stated that the decree had been given to me but that I had refused to sign a statement of acceptance.'

Archbishop McDonald glanced briefly at his book, but Horan accepted that a debate would not take place. Defiant, he gathered his papers and bid farewell to the two men.

Once outside, Horan immediately went on the attack.

Despite having twice walked out of the priesthood of his own accord, he was now vigorously challenging his dismissal. He told reporters he totally rejected the decree and, as far as he was concerned, he was still Father Neil Horan.

'I completely reject this decision,' he told the assembled Press. 'I appeal to the much higher court of heaven and the court of Jesus Christ. I now cannot preach, I cannot give out Communion. I am no more than a pagan. I feel it was unChristian and unCatholic.'

In subsequent interviews, Horan claimed 'they [the Catholic Church] are afraid of me and afraid of the Bible. They are afraid I will go into it too deeply and show up their beliefs.'

The media feasted on the controversy. At last it appeared that the Catholic Church had taken decisive action. Rome had its say on the most troublesome cleric to have come into the Church in decades. The official statement by Monsignor Moth confirmed that Horan had been laicised and could no longer carry out any ritual duties or be a priest in a diocese. The actual Vatican decree went much further, banning Horan from holding any office in a seminary or 'similar institution'. Effectively, Horan could not function in any institution which was under Church authority.

As news of the latest controversy concerning Horan spread, letters of support poured into his home in Nunhead as well as to his local newspaper, the *South London Press* – mainly from close acquaintances and former parishioners who had come to know Horan over the years in Southwark diocese. All the letters centred on the same issue; that Horan wasn't given a fair hearing and that it appeared that 'health grounds' were the reason for his dismissal. Among the personal letters of support received by Horan was one from the mother of the girl who had given evidence against him in his trial for gross indecency at the Old Bailey just three months earlier. Back in 1993, she had been one of those who encouraged him to relaunch his book, *A Glorious New World*. Her letter to Horan dated a week after he was sacked told the defrocked priest that she was 'horrified at what the Church has done'.

'Regardless of what they say, you are a good counsellor, a good speaker and a good writer,' she said. She enclosed a cheque to help Horan out.

Three weeks later, the mother wrote again in an effort to console the defrocked priest. This time, she told Horan that he proclaimed the Word of God and cared very much for people: 'The Church should be thankful. "Love thy neighbour" comes to mind. What about those who reported you to Rome? If they became ill, would they have to leave the priesthood?

'I realise I am not completely innocent but I do not want to be part of a Church that defrocks their priests, or any other leader for that matter, for not being well. Although I was horrible, I have learnt my lesson. Most people will still treat you as a priest. I hope things get better. God bless…'

In its editorial of 29 January, the *Irish Post* also rowed in behind the sacked cleric. It argued that everyone knew the name of the priest behind the Grand Prix and Olympics escapades, but few knew the name of the Archbishop who sacked him.

'Ex-Father Horan gave the best years of his life to the service of the Church. He does not deserve to be cast off like an old sock in his hour of need,' the editorial said.

The Survivors of Child Abuse (SOCA) group also joined the fray, accusing the Church of hypocrisy for defrocking Horan while allowing priests convicted of child sex-abuse continue to be members of the Church. Coordinator John Kelly told the *Star Sunday* newspaper: 'This raises many other questions. There are priests out there who have been convicted of committing the most heinous crimes against children yet for some reason the Catholic Church finds it very hard to take similar action against them. The only reason Father Horan is being defrocked is because this guy is a loose cannon and an obvious embarrassment to them.'

Reaction to Horan's dismissal at home in Ireland varied. To many, it was the final and inevitable chapter to Horan's years of controversial publicity stunts and public expression of heretical beliefs. Others believed that Horan was victimised simply because he was unwell.

Horan claims he found the greatest comfort in the support received from 'ordinary, decent people'. Horan knew Joan Daly from the time both of them attended primary school in Knockeenahone. Horan remembered her as an only child and 'an unusually friendly little girl, mad for talk'.

In the longest hand-written letter Horan ever received, Joan rekindled contact with her neighbour, encouraging him to ignore the critics and return to the priesthood – not in England, but at home in his native Scartaglen:

> Dear Neil
> I hope you are well since, as we are all fine here, thank God...
>
> We have all been watching you and reading about you in the papers in Ireland.
>
> Your home place behind has become a tourist attraction because I have shown people where the dancing priest is from. It is like God. There

is people for you and against you but no matter about that.

I know myself that you are right to make known about the Bible. I myself believe just as much as you do and even that you were friends with us I don't think that we ever discussed it. I have been telling everyone that I think we have got a lot of messages for the people lately, that we are living in the end times. But hopefully it won't end.

The world will go on in a new sinless way, as it seems to have been cursed since Adam-Eve disobeyed God at the start. They are supposed to have lost eternal life for their earthly bodies and for all of us by doing that. It goes to prove why Jesus became a human being and had a mother, to be like us. There can be no one greater than God who can do all works of creation.

Your adventures are yesterday's news already. But I personally think myself and I said the same to other people. You went the wrong way of getting the public attention because instead of drawing attention to God you drew attention to yourself the wrong way, because it made you look mad and irresponsible. By running out it gave you the wrong look.

The jail and that accusation about that child made it look a lot worse than the running out, which of course was very dangerous if it caused accidents. Don't worry about the jail part of it either. Sure I had an awful experience in jail and they got me transferred to a mental hospital in

Dublin about sixteen years ago over motor car insurance myself. Jail can be an experience.

There is great knowledge in religious books if they are read from ancient times. I have a lot of books I hope to take over to you…

I suppose that lies were always there too. A lie is dangerous and can sometimes go further than the truth. I hope that the woman was wrong about her child. But no matter a person can be tempted in many ways and any person can have a bad fault or a bad habit, but child abuse is bad. She may have been telling a lie or she thought she saw something or did she just want to put you down or what? I think myself it looked worse than the running out. I felt it wasn't true myself.

There is so many clergy taken to court now for child abuse. You should not have any contact with people going to your place. It is always safer in the eyes of the law. You were lucky not to be convicted of that. I don't know what your own crowd behind thought. I haven't met them lately. I will talk it out and let you know.

That *Star* [newspaper] paper fellow did not do you any favours with those pictures and that kind of a story. I read it that Sunday at Kearney's café. I think I got a shock. I took one of your Silverstone photos and put it near Our Lord's statue. I said it would help you.

I hope to get books from you when I go over. A lot of the old crowd are dead now. They would not be able to understand today's living. Don't worry about what people say or think. Sure I suppose everyone is entitled to their opinion.

That Archbishop is not doing you any favours. You are right not to give up. You should have signed your name to that letter as Father in the paper, and I think that you should always wear your priest collar because it shows you are a man of the cloth, as they say.

I don't agree too well with that dancing costume. I told you at my own house that it was not suitable. You should wear a black pants and your priest collar to make you look like a priest. I think army chaplains wear a collar with a uniform. It is such a loss to you and the people if you are not saying Mass, and I read that there is scarcity of priests in UK now, and they haven't got a parish priest in Scart [Scartaglen] lately as they had a Father Egan who got sick there and left some months ago. I saw a letter on the church wall from the bishop saying he did not have a full-time priest to replace him. You may laugh at this but I believe God intends to bring you back as far as Scart again as parish priest. There is a grand presbytery there also and plenty company. They have special lay prayer, people travelling long distances from other counties for Sunday evening prayer and healing every month with a few years.

Will you try to find a frame for my card and keep it as a souvenir. I got it in Tralee. I was going to write at Xmas. We don't hear from you. I suppose you don't go back but please God you will later. I intend having a few words with the bishop in Killarney on your behalf. If I don't go quick some other priest could have it. But you must let me know how you feel. It would be good enough for them all if you did get it. I imagine myself that God has it for you. I hope I am right.

There is a lot of changes over the years. I will have all the news for you when I visit, please God, maybe in April. I told Pat that you needed support. They probably don't really understand, I think, unless people read stories. Not many people read those kinds of books. We can learn a lot from reading religion…

God bless, Joan

In the wake of his showdown with the Vatican, Horan turned to some of the most unlikely people for support in his fight to have the decree overturned, among them Queen Elizabeth. Despite having come to the attention of the Buckingham Palace Intelligence Unit because of letters he had written to members of the Royal family a decade earlier, he planned a vigil outside the Palace, vowing to carry a placard that read, 'Your Majesty, please help me to fight the Vatican. It's a case of the Bible versus the Catholic Church now.'

Horan also openly challenged Archbishop McDonald to a public debate on the Bible, a challenge never taken up by the Archbishop or by anybody else from the Church.

The most reasoned appeal from Horan came by way of an open letter in which he argued that health issues were not a valid reason for being kicked out. One local newspaper in his native Kerry, *The Kingdom*, carried his letter in full. Horan wrote that, back in 1994, he sent a copy of his book to each of the four bishops of the Southwark diocese – the then Archbishop Michael Bowen and his three assistant bishops, Bishop Charles Henderson, Bishop John Jukes and Bishop Howard Tripp – as well as Monsignor John Hine, the Vicar General.

'Surely, I felt, if they thought there was anything seriously wrong in the book, they would point it out to me. What was their response? Nil. Only three of the bishops replied at all, and that was merely to acknowledge receipt. They held on to the books, although I told them to return them. They still have them.'

His newspaper letter also revealed that in October 2003, after Silverstone, Monsignor Richard Moth came to see him and requested that he voluntarily allow himself be defrocked. Horan agreed under one condition: that the Archbishop appoint an expert who would point out to him, from the Bible, where his beliefs were wrong. He got no response.

Horan's letter to the newspaper accepted he had gone too far at Silverstone and Athens. If the Archbishop and Monsignor had asked him, he said he would have made 'a solemn promise to never again break the law as part of my mission to promote the Bible'. 'Will I have to live forever with the sins of the Grand Prix and the marathon? Where is the forgiveness here?

'The official reason they gave for my defrocking was the poor state of my health. Is poor health a valid reason to be thrown out of the priesthood? Is it valid in Canon law? Surely, any Christian church should look after its sick members, even more than the healthy ones, rather than throwing them out?

'A priest friend told me recently my millennial beliefs have been regarded as heresy by some within the church. If that is the case, surely the very least they should have done was to have let me know this in writing?

'Why did they give health as the reason? Was it because they were afraid to give the real reason? Afraid that they could not prove my writings wrong?'

For months, Horan remained courteous to the Church hierarchy in his public statements about what had happened but he was getting nowhere in his bid to have the decision reversed. In May 2006, the sacked priest changed tactics. He launched a scathing public attack on Pope Benedict XVI, just weeks after his election as head of the Catholic Church. Horan's open letter to the Pontiff, sent to media all over the UK and Ireland, was accompanied by a notice of his intention to picket the Apostolic Nunciature in Wimbledon, home of the Papal Nuncio.

The letter held the Pope personally responsible for Horan's dismissal. As the main signatory on the decree, it was Cardinal Ratzinger, as he was then, who did the Pope's dirty work. But Horan took grave issue with the fact that the late Pope John Paul had been 'dragged into' the whole affair and that the decree had claimed he had 'heard the merits of the case' and had given it 'careful consideration'. Horan said he didn't believe a word of this. He argued that Pope John Paul was too sick to take any decision and was in no fit state to consider any of his case.

Furthermore, Monsignor Moth had written two letters to the Vatican about Horan. But Horan was not told of this at the time and at no stage were the accusations made against Horan given to him in writing. Commonsense, he said, not to mind Canon law, should have ensured that this was how things were done.

But what irked Horan most was the reference in the Vatican decree to the possibility of him abusing children. The decree stated: 'Ordinary [bishop] must all the more be exercised even if there is the remotest chance of the priest abusing minors.'

Horan accused Pope Benedict of slander because these words

were written on 15 October 2004 – ten days before his trial for gross indecency opened at the Old Bailey. 'I have never abused a minor in my life,' Horan told the Pope. 'The very mention of child abuse is a slur on me, given the explosive meaning which those two words have taken on in recent years.

'You wrote those words ten days before my trial began. How could you possibly comment, one way or the other, before the trial was over?'

The letter left Pope Benedict in no doubt about how Horan felt. He accused the Church of hypocrisy, naming one priest who had been jailed for five years after sexually abusing fifty boys. This priest was never defrocked. He told the Pontiff he was taking him to the European Court of Justice on two charges: unfair dismissal and defamation of character.

'See you in court, Your Holiness,' the letter said.

Horan was fighting a losing battle. His grievances were never aired in the European Court of Justice and the Church authorities remained silent about them. Horan refuses to accept the decision and feels he is still entitled to call himself 'Father'.

But even members of his family struggled to understand why Horan was so determined to remain a priest, having gone to such lengths over the years to get out of the Church. His brother Dan welcomed the move by the Vatican to dismiss his brother from the priesthood. He told the *Star* newspaper he hoped the defrocking would put an end to 'the silly stunts like Athens and Silverstone because he doesn't have the novelty value of being in the priesthood'.

Dan Horan and others hoped in vain. Collar or no collar, Neil Horan's publicity campaign wasn't finished yet. Not by a long shot.

11

HEIL HITLER

The German authorities never got it so easy. They were made fully aware of the ex-priest's imminent arrival in Berlin to pull off yet another publicity stunt at the 2006 World Cup finals when letters and press releases sent from Horan himself arrived through the letterboxes of police and football chiefs. Among the recipients were the chief of Berlin police, the German Ambassador to the UK, the President and the Chancellor of the Federal Republic of Germany, the Chairman of the German Football Association and FIFA bosses.

Horan detailed his intention to travel to Germany. They could expect the Grand Prix and Olympic priest in town any day soon. He planned to stage a demonstration outside Berlin's Olympic Stadium on the day of the World Cup final in support of Adolf Hitler, a man whom Horan claimed was a good leader and part of God's grand plan.

There was an expected worldwide TV audience of more than 700 million viewers for the World Cup final. The publicity potential was enormous, bigger than anything Horan had attempted before.

While the Athens and Silverstone stunts had caused offence to many, the Berlin trip posed a far more sinister threat. Horan had become an expert on UK laws pertaining to public order and demonstrations. However, he knew nothing about how the Germans might view his publicity stunts.

Three years earlier, in 2003, Horan had been slated by the Three Faiths Forum, a movement founded to encourage goodwill and friendship between Muslims, Christians and Jews. Horan had issued a statement claiming that all suicide bombers were sent by Christ and attacks on Israel made him happy because the Israelis 'are far away from God'. But, luckily for Horan, the statement received relatively little publicity and appeared to pass under the public radar.

Now, the pro-Nazi gig had the potential to be the most risky and ludicrous stunt to date with the potential to cause grave offence to millions. It was also likely to land the ex-priest with another stint in prison.

Horan wanted to claim publicly that the Holocaust was the will of God, sent to punish the Jews for 'mixing too much with the Gentiles when they should have always kept themselves separate, as God's chosen people.'

He argued that Moses foretold 3500 years of Jewish history, in Chapter 28 of *Deuteronomy*. The first fourteen verses listed the blessings that would come to them if they obeyed God, the rest of the chapter outlined the curses that would come upon them if they disobeyed.

Horan told media and police bosses that, 'since the Jews disobeyed far more than they obeyed, the curses are what generally came to them'.

Horan's Ryanair flight touched down at Schönefeld Airport in Berlin shortly after 9pm. It was 6 July 2006 and the country was gripped by World Cup final fever.

Totally oblivious to what was about to come, Horan stepped off the plane. He had no sooner set foot on the tarmac than four police officers surrounded him, arresting him on foot of a warrant obtained on suspicion of promoting national socialism. He was escorted straight to police headquarters in Berlin where he was locked away in a cell overnight.

He had been warned. Police officers in the UK subsequently claimed that they gave Horan ample advance warning about German law and what could happen if he went ahead.

Prior to setting off for Berlin, Horan had written to police in Southwark, giving details of what he planned to do. By that stage, he was a familiar face to many of the police, including those who dealt exclusively with anti-social behaviour orders (ASBOs).

An ASBO had been slapped on Horan in 2005, preventing him from going anywhere near the London Marathon. Local police and civil authorities in London wanted to avoid another Athens-Olympics-type fiasco. But Horan insisted on doing his peace jig on the day of the marathon, albeit some distance from the marathon route. Police officers called to his house that morning and accompanied him to the corner of Tanner Street and Tower Bridge Road. A reporter from the *Southwark News* summed up his efforts days later, describing how 'the ghetto blaster boomed into life with a cheery Irish jig and Father Horan jigged, jumped and kicked, arms by his side and face straight, kilt adorned with the star of David flying up to reveal bright green underpants, until tired, he came to a stop'.

Police and the Southwark Council claimed they advised Horan that the Berlin stunt was in a whole new league. Laws pertaining to support for Hitler in Germany were far stricter than in the UK, and they claimed he was advised not to go.

Horan accepts that he was told about the German laws but categorically denies he was ever advised not to travel to Berlin.

In a subsequent ASBO application to have Horan banned

from the London marathon, Sergeant James Kenny-Levick of Southwark police station claimed he received literature from Horan prior to the Berlin trip that 'alarmed him very much'.

He said the literature 'contained strong views based on complex religious interpretations of the Bible, stating that the destiny of the Jewish race was pre-ordained, thus making the Holocaust inevitable and Hitler a servant of God'.

Sergeant Kenny-Levick said he 'strongly advised [Horan]that although the British police couldn't prevent his trip, his actions would contravene strict German laws forbidding Holocaust denial and promotion of the Nazi movement...I also tried to convey the potential distress that expounding his ideas might cause to a multi-national audience and the potential public order consequences. I was disappointed Mr Horan did not heed my advice.'

By lunchtime on the day after he was apprehended at Schönefeld Airport, Horan was in a prison van on his way to Berlin's Moabit penitentiary. It was home to about 1400 prisoners, many of them hardened criminals and killers.

The German police had confiscated everything that Horan had, including his dancing kilt. But the poster he had prepared and the documents he had in his suitcase would form the real basis of their case against him. In their view, Horan's planned stunt and the writing on his posters contravened German law by amounting to approval of acts committed under National Socialism.

Horan had a number of posters written in large black marker, each measuring roughly a metre square. One read: 'In Memorium Adolf Hitler, A Great Leader, 1889-1945'; others read: 'Adolf Hitler Was a Good Leader, Says the Bible', 'Adolf Hitler Was Raised Up by Christ To Punish the Jews, Says the

Bible' and 'Auschwitz Was Good: It Led to the Birth Of Israel, Says the Bible'.

For the following nine weeks, Horan was locked away inside Moabit prison awaiting trial. Things were different in Moabit from Woodhill, where he had served time after the Silverstone stunt. Few of the warders or inmates spoke any English and Horan struggled to communicate. Orders to change sheets or towels, announced over the prison's public address system, had to be translated for him.

He was lucky to be placed in a cell next door to Uwe Karl, who spoke relatively good English. Karl also translated letters Horan received from prison authorities, some of them responses to written requests for postage stamps or permission to join German language classes.

Unlike Woodhill, all meals in Moabit were delivered to the cells. Prisoners exercised every day but apart from this hour, it was close to twenty-three-hour daily lockdown.

Tea was delivered at 2.30pm every day and this was the last time the inmates saw any human being, apart from their cellmate, until 7am the following morning.

But what struck Horan most of all in Moabit was his anonymity. In Woodhill, practically every one of the inmates knew who he was. In Moabit, he was nobody, something that Horan claimed made his term in prison 'much easier, as when you are the centre of attention in any group it can put a great strain on you.'

If letting Horan stew in prison for a few weeks was the German authorities' strategy for dealing with his capers, it appears to have worked. He found the twenty-three-hour daily lockdown a 'huge and insurmountable obstacle': 'You felt cabined, cribbed, confined, bound in. You felt as if the world did not exist outside the four walls of your cell. It was a feeling of hopelessness and helplessness that no words could describe.

'You heard the clatter of keys all day long. Since then, the word freedom has taken on a value and power that it did not remotely have before.'

On 6 September, Horan was taken from Moabit prison to stand trial. But it was a trial that never got underway. He was released from custody and sent back to the UK. He claims his solicitor and the police had told him his trial would never go ahead and that he would be released on the day of his only court appearance in Berlin.

On the day of his release, two police officers met Horan at the gates of Moabit prison. They accompanied him to an Internet cafe where he booked an Easyjet flight to Stansted. Horan's parting memories of Berlin were positive, especially when he recalls that the two officers 'bought coffee and cakes for me'.

'They took me on a guided tour of Berlin in their car, with the two of them taking it in turns to explain the sights to me. Finally, they dropped me off at the airport and left me in the care of a colleague who was on duty at the airport. He stayed with me until I went into the departure lounge.'

As with Silverstone and Athens, Horan reflected on his actions. He told one London newspaper he felt some of his posters were 'very badly worded and wide open to misunderstanding'. He also said he would consider never using the same posters again as part of his mission.

While most of the media listed Horan's record in breaking the law, none highlighted him breaking his own word. Immediately after Athens, he told police, journalists and the general public that he would never again interrupt a sporting event or break the law.

His promise was made clearest of all in the letter he sent to Vanderlei de Lima after he robbed him of gold in Athens two years before.

He wrote to the Brazilian athlete: 'I have now successfully completed the double witness on the world stage, at Silverstone and Athens. I have put the Bible where it deserves to be, on the highest platforms on earth. I have completed my mission.

'I can honestly say, with God as my witness, I will never break the law again, anywhere in the world. If I do, I invite any who are present, when it happens, to attack me, with fist, shoe, elbow, fingernails, or weapons, because that is what I would deserve. I would deserve to be shot on sight. I would not deserve to live.'

Horan still feels aggrieved at the German authorities for jailing him, without trial, in a country he had barely set foot in.

And he feels aggrieved that German authorities are still 'illegally holding on to his property', including his national costume.

Luckily for Horan, the German authorities either didn't read his pledge never again to break the law or didn't take it seriously. Somebody must have felt that shooting Horan on sight wasn't quite the answer.

By the following year, Horan's demonstrations appeared to be running out. Southwark Council moved to have another ASBO put on the turbulent resident. He was forced to replace his dance costume after the Berlin episode and, wearing a new orange kilt, green waistcoat and socks, Horan arrived at Camberwell Green Magistrates Court on 13 April 2007. He accepted an interim order banning him from entering any of the boroughs along the race route on the day of the London Marathon, 22 April.

One month later, the council was back in court looking for something more substantial. They wanted a more permanent end put to Horan's antics around the city of London, especially on London Marathon day when he was most likely to strike.

A schedule of incidents was prepared for court by Southwark Council, detailing several of Horan's demonstrations that, it was claimed, posed a public order threat. Silverstone, Athens and Berlin were listed on the council dossier, but several of the claims relating to other controversial demonstrations infuriated Horan.

The dossier stated he was 'spotted by police outside the Lebanese Embassy on 16 December 2006 carrying placards which read, "Jesus Christ Supports Hezbollah".

Horan claimed that this gave a false impression of him turning up unannounced. He had, in fact, got full permission from the police for the demonstration and was observed by police while he carried it out. And his placard said that Jesus Christ was 'directing' Hezbollah, not 'supporting' it. Jesus doesn't take sides, he said.

The dossier also claimed that in June 2004, at the Epsom Derby, 'Horan was spotted by police and tackled, moments before they believed he was about to run in front of the horses'.

Horan described this charge as 'another hairy [hoary] old lie'. He claimed he never intended running in front of the horses and that police never put a hand on him. He was arrested but released without charge and had, on four subsequent occasions, arrived at Epsom with a police escort to do his peace dance.

The ASBO was ultimately made against Horan, banning him from going anywhere near the Tour de France cycle race in London that year and the vicinity of the London Marathon up to 2010.

But he claimed the outcome a victory because an application to have him get written permission from sporting event organisers before being admitted was rejected.

So was an application to ban him carrying 'any placard in a public place that causes or is likely to cause harassment, alarm or distress'.

'I'm free to go on proclaiming my message,' Horan said afterwards.

And he did. With a minor victory under his belt, Horan danced on. Over the next two years he continued his demonstrations, taking his peace jig to locations all over the UK.

His media campaign also continued. He issued press statements ahead of demonstrations at locations such as the French Embassy in London, informing Tour de France supporters that, 'The French are the frogs foretold in the Bible,' and that, 'France has played a big part in fulfilling Bible prophecy.'

Despite his brushes with the law, Horan refused to soften the tone of his messages and public statements.

Horan challenged the Palestinian Ambassador to a wrestling match on 17 October 2007 on the footpath outside the Palestinian office in Hammersmith, London. He claimed that the ambassador had blasphemed two years earlier by calling God a criminal. Horan's challenge to the ambassador to publicly debate Zionism fell on deaf ears. Accordingly, Horan said he was now challenging him to combat.

'My poster will read: "This is the Palestinian office. Its director is Professor Manuel Hassassian. He openly insulted me in Trafalgar Square. I challenge him to come out and wrestle me. If he refuses, he is a coward and a twit."'

In June 2008, Horan returned to the Epsom Derby, transported by jeep and accompanied by Surrey police. In July of the same year, he joined the London Gay March to publicly 'call on Jesus to sort out the world's mess'. His press release asked Jesus: 'Why are you hiding yourself in Heaven? What is the point letting the world drift aimlessly on any longer?

'You know that the majority of the learned classes believe and teach that we humans came from the monkey. It totally contradicts your teaching and your father's.'

Seemingly out of trouble and with a marked fall-off in the level of publicity he was receiving, Horan believed it was time to up his game.

With major sporting occasions no longer a realistic option, a new direction was required. The dancing priest was bound for the Hammersmith Apollo.

12

NEIL'S GOT TALENT

Piers Morgan smirked and looked at the Hammersmith Apollo audience in delight. Amanda Holden clapped along in amusement. Simon Cowell chewed his pen and rolled his eyes to heaven in disbelief.

Horan danced his underpants off in front of thousands at the Hammersmith Apollo. He had successfully passed the first audition stage of ITV's *Britain's Got Talent* competition, 2009, and was now performing his soft jig in front of TV cameras and millions of viewers all over the UK and Ireland.

The talent show thrives on the weird and wonderful and Horan fitted the bill perfectly. Standing at the microphone, centre-stage, Horan proudly told Amanda Holden his name and his age – sixty-one.

An Irish jig blared out through the sound system and Horan took off on stage. Repeatedly turning in circles, he tapped right toe in front of left foot up to fifteen times before changing to tapping left toe in front of right foot. It was a version of a soft jig all of its own but the Apollo crowd went berserk and rose to their feet.

True to form, Cowell ignored the audience reaction and shot from the hip: 'I thought it was a little bit limited. You did only dance in a circle. I'm going to say "No."'

Morgan took the populist route: 'This guy represents every folk dancer in the country, and I for one am going to say "Yes."'

Holden rowed in behind the former newspaper editor and gave another "Yes." The dancing priest had won over two of the three judges, enough to see him through to the next round.

But over the days that followed the TV broadcast of the audition, it wasn't Horan's twinkle toes that dominated the media coverage. Millions had seen the audition and recognised the dancer for who he really was.

This wasn't just any sixty-one year-old looking for one last shot at fame. It was the crackpot cleric from Silverstone and Athens who had been jailed twice and kicked out of the Catholic Church for warning that a nuclear holocaust was very soon to come.

The newspapers reported that Horan had left TV bosses red-faced as they weren't aware of his dodgy past. The Irish *Daily Mirror* boasted an exclusive by revealing the man who had appeared on TV to millions over the mid-May weekend was, in fact, a defrocked priest.

But the paper also wrongly claimed that Horan had ruined the Atlanta Olympics and had been cleared of indecently assaulting a seven-year-old girl. Horan was never near the Atlanta Olympics and was never charged with indecent assault.

Horan was quoted in the *Mirror* as saying the programme producers knew full well who he was and that he suspected they wanted him to pull another publicity stunt just to boost ratings. 'I think they wanted me to jump into Amanda Holden's lap,' he joked.

But he claimed he had refrained from doing anything over-the-top because he was proud to represent Ireland and to show off his folk dancing. He did warn, however, that if he was invited back to perform again, he might 'have something up his sleeve'.

Speculation soon turned to the judges after Horan's televised performance. An editorial in the *Irish World* questioned how journalist Piers Morgan and his two judge colleagues could not have known the background to the troubled former priest.

'Of course, Piers Morgan and his fellow judges must have known about Father Horan's past,' the editorial stated. 'And it was no doubt with that in mind and the fact his TV appearance would provoke newspaper headlines that they allowed him on to the programme and voted him through to the next round.'

The producers and the judges never definitively said that any of them knew exactly who Horan was. A *Britain's Got Talent* spokesperson was quoted as saying, 'Neil attended auditions to display his talent at Irish dancing. At no point during filming did he show any other motivation for anything other than dancing'.

As far as they were concerned, Horan came to dance and that's what he did. No placards, no leaflets, no speeches or stunts. Just an Irish soft jig.

Horan is in no doubt that everybody involved with the programme knew in advance who he was. After all, he had told them all about his sins months before his audition was ever shown on TV. He had filled up an application form to enter the talent show and taken it along to the first audition at the Earl's Court in London. One section of the form asked applicants to send all photos of themselves that had appeared in newspapers and magazines. Horan's written reply to this was, 'It would be impossible for me to do this, as my photo was in the Press all over the world after Silverstone and Athens.'

He handed the application to one of the preliminary judges at Earl's Court. Before he did his jig at the first audition, he claims the female judge questioned him for several minutes about his work. He informed the judge he was a priest but that he had been defrocked by the Catholic Church. He said he was kicked out because of his beliefs about the second coming of Christ but also because of what had happened at Silverstone and Athens.

The day before the Hammersmith Apollo audition on 27 January, researcher David Jones rang Horan. When Jones asked about Silverstone and the reasons for the stunt, Horan was happy to explain but immediately worried it would signal the end of his talent show bid. It didn't.

Series producer Ben Thursby also rang Horan about a month before the audition was shown on TV. Horan claims he confessed to Thursby that he was a controversial figure, but he was assured by the producer that every contestant was taken on his or her merits. Horan claimed afterwards, 'The producers had a full six months between the Earl's Court audition and the screening of my performance on television. Surely time enough to investigate what exactly Silverstone and Athens were.'

As for the judges, Horan claims that Piers Morgan, at least, should have known who he was. Horan had sent Morgan, a former editor of the *Daily Mirror*, leaflets about his beliefs. Morgan sent at least one written acknowledgement in July 1999.

Opinion divided over Horan's appearance on *Britain's Got Talent*. For some, it represented a proud Irishman in his sixties being given a shot at the big-time. For others, it was exploitation of a mentally unstable ex-priest.

Some writers questioned how a former priest who had given the best years of his life to the Church could now be reduced to such a sorry state, a national joke.

Irish Daily Mail columnist Brenda Power went further. In her column of 19 May 2009, she said a child of three would have to spend only a couple of minutes in the company of 'Father' Neil

Horan before realising he was 'away with the fairies'. It simply wasn't credible, she said, that the researchers and producers of *Britain's Got Talent* didn't know what they were doing when they let Horan out on stage before a huge television audience.

The most perfunctory enquiry about his recent public performances would have elicited the fact that he danced his bizarre little jig for the cameras during the G20 summit protests in London just weeks earlier, and this alone ought to have set alarm bells ringing. 'If the show genuinely was what it purports to be – a selection process to find talent good enough to entertain the Queen at a royal command performance – Neil Horan wouldn't have got within an ass's roar of the stage,' she wrote.

Power's hard-hitting article ultimately accused the judges and the programme producers of bullying. She wrote that whoever decided to put Horan on television knew he couldn't dance to save his life but fully realised that his bizarre efforts and his misguided hopes of stardom would provide a brief and amusing diversion. Any concern for his mental fragility or ability to withstand humiliation was overridden by the prospect of a cheap laugh, Power said.

Needless to say, Horan didn't quite see it that way. He admitted he was no Michael Flatley but argued if the crowd reaction in the Hammersmith Apollo was anything to go by, he should be given a chance to progress to the next round.

Despite several newspapers reporting that Horan had qualified for the semi-finals by being given the thumbs-up at the Apollo, that's not what transpired. Nine days after the Hammersmith audition, Horan and other contenders were taken to Lancaster House near Buckingham Palace to find out if they had made it through to the semi-finals. Contestants were required to go before the judges in groups, but were not asked to audition again. Cowell, Morgan and Holden were seated together. It was Holden who dished out the bad news that, by a unanimous verdict, Horan had not made it through.

The dancing priest was gutted. While the Bible had taken centre-stage all his life, his devotion to traditional music and particularly Irish dancing remained very strong.

Among all the jigs he had done – including those purely for entertainment purposes around the UK and Ireland – the audience reaction in Hammersmith to this particular soft jig was unparalleled. Horan claimed that Amanda Holden told him at one stage during the auditions that the Hammersmith Apollo hadn't rocked to the same extent since Tina Turner took to the stage. He even suggested to presenters Ant and Dec that Irish dancing was under-represented on TV and called for a Eurovision-type contest for folk dancing.

Horan rallied family and friends to back his appeal to continue on his new-found journey to stardom. They bombarded the judges and the producers with letters, appealing for one more chance for Horan.

His brother Dan wrote from Kerry, emphasising how much time Neil had devoted to practising every day, ever since he was told he would be auditioning in front of the cameras.

His landlady of thirteen years, Delia McManus, claimed she knew Neil Horan better than anyone. She said that she 'never saw [Horan] so down as when he was told on 7 February that he hadn't made it through. And she promised that, although she was eighty-nine, she would go to see him perform if he was allowed through to the semi-finals.

Kathleen Mullin, a close acquaintance of Horan, told how she sat in the audience at the Hammersmith Apollo for about six hours that day, but, 'Neil's act was the best of the lot…please find it in your hearts to give him a place in the semi-finals'.

Sophie Hicks, another close acquaintance of Horan and a former ballet dancer, wrote exclusively to Amanda Holden, claiming the interaction between the dancing priest and the audience at the Hammersmith Apollo was 'on a par with that of a contemporary pop star'. And she told the judge that because Horan was 'getting on' and 'can't go on forever', he deserved another chance.

A spokesperson for Talkback Thames, the company that produced the talent show, was right when she told one newspaper that the 'judges' decision was final and any appeal was highly unlikely to be successful.' The begging letters all fell on deaf ears.

For a while, it seemed as if the years of daily dance practice had gone for nothing. The Queen would never get to see the dancing priest perform, at least not by invitation to the Royal command performance. But Horan's TV appearance on *Britain's Got Talent* didn't entirely go to waste. His performance featured on YouTube and continues to be viewed by thousands.

One by one, the invitations to perform at charity functions and variety shows around Ireland and the UK began to arrive. Few really knew or cared what he had to say about Bible prophecy, but many appeared fascinated by a sixty-one-year-old defrocked priest who wore a kilt and danced an Irish jig.

Among the invitations was one from an amateur theatre company in Croydon that planned a cabaret featuring stand-up comics, magicians and jugglers. A number of different acts were to perform music and comedy at a small venue in the Fairfield Halls in Croydon on 4 June 2010.

The organisers believed that Horan would fit the bill perfectly as they wanted to 'avoid the musical bits being too serious because it is a Friday night audience and they will be having a few drinks and hopefully in a chilled-out mood.'

The organisers wanted the infamous former cleric to sit down in front of the audience after he finished dancing for a Jonathan Ross or David Letterman-style interview to discuss Athens and his run-in with the Pope. They promised him that the audience would love him, just like the audience at *Britain's Got Talent*.

The Croydon organisers said they hadn't much money but were willing to pay his expenses and 'sort out some booze'. Horan hardly ever drinks and if he does he takes a glass of wine.

He is glad to oblige whenever he can so the dancing priest show goes on – Trafalgar Square, charity events, pub openings, weddings and birthday parties.

But Horan is more drawn to the big stage. In January 2010, he wrote to Danny Jordaan, Chief of the 2010 World Cup Organising Committee, introducing himself as the '*Britain's Got Talent* Irish dancer'. He asked Jordaan to allow him to perform his peace dance at the World Cup opening or closing ceremony in South Africa. Horan claimed that allowing him do his peace dance in South Africa would be 'a lovely gesture' towards the Irish people in view of the outrage that had engulfed the country two months earlier, when a hand ball by Thierry Henry denied Ireland a place in the World Cup finals.

Horan was peeved at not having heard back from the World Cup boss. He appealed to even higher authority, making his case to South African President Jacob Zuma:

> Dear President Jacob
> Warmest Christian greetings to you, your family, your staff and the people of the Republic of South Africa...
>   I enclose a copy of a letter which I sent three

months ago to Danny Jordaan. I received no reply, not even an acknowledgement of my letter, and that from a native son of South Africa. No sign of the renowned African hospitality here.

I appeal to Your Excellency: Please intervene on my behalf and do all you can to have my request dealt with.

If I receive no positive reply, I plan, with God's help, to go to South Africa and perform on the streets of Pretoria and Johannesburg during the World Cup – if I can raise the necessary money...

But Horan's plans to take his dance to a world stage didn't stop there. He wanted to return to, of all places, the racing circuit where he once caused mayhem, as a result of which he ended up in jail. In a letter written in April 2010 to Formula One Chief Bernie Ecclestone, Horan claimed the timing was ideal for his sins of the past to be forgiven and asked if he could return to the British Grand Prix:

My dear Bernie

Warmest greetings to you, your family, your staff and everyone associated with Formula One racing. I wish you well in your life and career.

By the time of this year's British Grand Prix, it will be all of seven years since I intervened at the Hangar Straight in Silverstone.

Seven is the most perfect of all numbers in the Bible because of the creation of the world in seven days – the six days of creation plus the seventh day of rest. That is why we have a seven-day week.

I request that I be admitted to this year's Silverstone Grand Prix and I believe you, above anyone else, could make this possible for me…

I would be happy to call up to Prince's Gate to talk over the issue face-to-face.

What I would like to do is this: perform my peace dance in front of the Grand Stand just before the start of the Grand Prix. It only takes two minutes. I would have a poster with the words 'Peace Dance for the Silverstone Grand Prix by the *Britain's Got Talent* Irish Dancer', and on the other side, 'Salute to Formula One and the Enjoyment It Brings the World'.

It would be a fitting and happy end to the chapter that began on 20 July 2003, which had a huge effect on my life. People still keep saying to me: 'You could have caused a dreadful accident.'

Indeed I could, but all is well that ends well…

Five days later, Ecclestone replied, acknowledging the dancing priest's request. He told Horan he was forwarding his letter to the Formula One race director who is 'responsible for the sporting aspects'. 'I am sure he will contact you to discuss your proposal,' Ecclestone said.

To date, Horan has not heard if he will return to the Grand Prix. Despite all that happened seven years ago, he remains hopeful of a positive outcome. While he waits, weddings and charity function appearances will have to suffice.

13

THE WAITING GAME

In 1994, journalist Robert Chalmers of the *Observer* sat down in a Dartford cafe to interview Horan. They discussed Horan's book, *A Glorious New World*, and, of course, the Bible.

The troubled priest sipped a sherry as he told Chalmers how the merchants of Tarshish in Ezekiel's Biblical writings were the British, and that the Queen is mentioned in the Old Testament. And with no hint of irony, he explained that Biblical references to 'frogs' meant the French, and that the three spirits like frogs (*Revelation* 16) refer to Liberty, Equality and Fraternity'.

Chalmers's subsequent article briefly explained Horan's brush with the psychiatric profession, wondering what a secular psychiatrist would make of millennarians such as Billy Graham and Ronald Reagan, or even the Pope, 'especially if he happened to let slip that he drinks the blood of Christ and is the chosen representative of God on earth'.

Horan, Chalmers wrote, 'strikes you as a man unusually affected by suffering; someone whose powerful desire to do good has combined explosively with an unsophisticated approach to texts, whether they be the Bible or Irish ballads of his childhood.'

Horan explained that, at that time, he might be allowed back to his parish in Nunhead, if only he'd stop talking about Armageddon. But, as he pointed out to the journalist, the conviction that all humanity is about to be blown to smithereens isn't the easiest thought to put to the back of your mind. He was waiting for the second coming, which he was sure was not too far away.

Sixteen years on, little has changed. Horan still seems to fit Chalmers's description of a man who 'struggles to exist on social security, wandering a strange limbo; desperately missing his parishioners, but unable to resist the urgent call of his predictions.'

In a small house on Howbury Road in Nunhead, Horan continues to sit and wait. He waits for replies to written requests to perform his peace jig at major sporting events like the World Cup in South Africa and the British Grand Prix.

He waits for responses from significant political and religious leaders to his latest writings on aspects of Biblical prophecy.

More than anything, he waits for the second coming of Jesus Christ, something he believes in now with more conviction than ever before, despite all that has happened throughout his controversial and sometimes outrageous life.

Horan lives peacefully with his landlady of fourteen years, Delia McManus. A kind and religious woman in her ninetieth year, she has become family to Horan. She 'tells him off like a child', now and again, but would never throw him out. She believes he has done his penance for his wrongdoings, but the Bible is always right and Neil is right to say so.

He studies and reads the Scriptures every day, highlighting their significance and relevance to current world events. He is at pains to point out he is not a prophet and doesn't hear voices. He is merely interpreting the Bible. He continues to justify his actions, although sorry he went as far as he did on several occasions. It's the Bible that counts, he says, not Neil Horan.

But those around Horan struggle to understand how he has never fully grasped the concept of leverage. Having gained massive world-wide publicity, how could he have failed to use it more effectively to spread his message?

He admits that the messenger has become better known than the message, something that, he says, saddens him greatly: 'My being famous is not automatically a clash with the message being famous. The fame of the one could help the fame of the other. They need not be mutually exclusive.

'So far, the fame of the messenger far outweighs the fame of the message. I have done, and am doing, everything in my power to change it. My message is all about a kingdom, a kingdom of 1000 years, which Christ will set up over all the earth at his coming. It is not well known. It is not known at all by the vast bulk of mankind. I wish it were different. However, it would be untrue to say that the message has not got through at all.'

A self-declared iconoclast, Horan rebels against 'false religious teaching, false teaching about the Bible, attacks on the Bible, false teaching about life and ways of the world I consider to challenge the Bible's position.' He is, by his own admission, 'a fundamentalist in the true sense of the word.'

Only one religion holds the truth, he believes, and that is Judaism. True Christianity is Judaism, with Jesus at its centre. All other religions are man-made, composed of human ideas and doctrines. He also has enormous respect for Islam and believes that the West has much to learn from what it teaches. He is convinced that Islamic fundamentalists are often misunderstood and misrepresented by the media. 'One man's terrorist is another man's freedom fighter,' he says.

Thirty-five years after he first walked into the Christadelphian lecture in Dartford, Horan continues to write extensively on the

Bible. His writings vary from brief synopses of particular Biblical themes to more detailed pamphlets and essays. He is clearly more at ease with complex theological, political or sociological issues than with everyday life.

Daily routine still includes Irish dance practice, a jog or two and a nightly cup of Ovaltine. He continues to carry out 'social calls', helping those he empathises with or who appear to have lost their way in life.

Most weeks, he sees about ten people he has come to know over the years and to whom is now an unofficial counsellor. Among them is a mother of a suicide victim, a bereaved widow and a rape victim struggling to form meaningful relationships with men fourteen years after her ordeal. Most of those he counsels suffer from depression, something Horan himself admits has been part of his whole adult life.

For most people who know him, Horan is a mass of contradictions. The shy and unassuming Kerryman can leave his simple abode on Howbury Road and become transformed into a publicity-seeking stuntman at the far end of the world.

His analysis of scripture can be detailed and complex, yet the personal greeting cards he sends to friends and acquaintances are often hand-drawn and decorated with coloured markers, more befitting an infant than a sixty-two-year-old Biblical scholar. Discussion on existentialism or world politics comes easy, yet the comfort of small-talk has eluded him since childhood.

At all times Horan comes across to friend and foe as courteous, decent and kind. Yet the people closest to Horan, like Derek Hilsden, the man who befriended Horan the day he walked into the Chirstadelphian lecture in 1974, describes Horan as 'a very careful and shrewd manipulator'.

'Who else could have manipulated the BBC and the Press in

the way he has done to get the coverage he did?' he asks. And no, he's not mad, says Hilsden. Far from it.

'Some of his behaviour is bizarre but because his beliefs mean more to him than his own life, that moves his actions from stupid to courageous. He's got a very fine mind and if he concentrated it in the way I feel we could have been doing things legitimately together, he probably would have made more impact in drawing people to what we believe.'

Nobody among those who are close to Horan justifies or supports his Silverstone and Athens publicity stunts. Practically all the character references supplied at his gross indecency trial at the Old Bailey went out of their way to distance themselves from these actions. Yet all the references spoke of a kind man who has, over the entirety of his life, done a share of good.

Patrick Jones from County Clare wrote that the controversial cleric had brought happiness to his life and remained someone he could 'turn to in times of need'.

Elizabeth Clifford described a man who was 'a deep thinker, highly intelligent and learned with a wonderful simplicity'. Elizabeth was a sacristan while Horan was a priest at St Thomas's parish in Nunhead. While she disapproved of Horan's publicity antics, she stood firm in her belief that Horan was 'a man of faith and conviction with admirable Christian qualities'.

And there's Teresa Lennon, originally from County Tipperary but living in London and a regular visitor to Horan's home on Howbury Road. She's convinced that Horan loves the limelight; that he's an attention-seeker who does things that 'just don't make sense'. 'People think he's a nutter; honestly, he's got an awful obsession.' Yet she, too, 'loves him to bits and would do anything for him'.

Horan admits he has an addiction to publicity. His defence

has always remained the same. 'I believe some ends do justify the means...I want publicity for the greatest book in the world, the holy Bible, and the vital message of the coming of Christ.'

Millions beg to differ. The public knows Horan as nothing more than a dancing nutter and a fool, a crazed lunatic who is a self-publicist, deranged to the point where he is a public danger and whose mad-hatter stunts cause great harm to innocent people, notably Brazilian marathoner Vanderlei de Lima.

Horan questions the media's view of him. 'A farce and a joke? You must be joking. I do accept, though, that my jig is just that for some who genuinely hold that view. They are, I believe, a small minority.'

'My message is fierce weighty and serious. Is there not a place, side by side with it, for the lighter side? My costume and my dance are aimed to bring fun and enjoyment to people. They are aimed to bring a little joy to this vale of tears. They are meant to represent the lighter side of life, as a balance to the heavier side of life which my message stands for.

'When I see the joy on children's faces, when I see children imitating my steps, in places like Trafalgar Square, it convinces me that my dance does make this world a better place – better by a tiny margin, maybe, but better nevertheless.

'With all due respect, I would safely say that our words have very little effect on young children, but my dance does. Neither do our words have much effect on people who have no command of English, but my dance does.

'I have a little box which was given to me by a Korean child last year. It had tasty chocolate in it. It has Korean writing on it. Neither the child nor the mother could say anything to me in English, but they could appreciate my dance.

'At the Iraq War Inquiry in January, a Chinese child handed

me Chinese dried bread, wrapped in paper with Chinese writing on it. He handed it to me while I danced.'

Horan doesn't deliver lectures in spacious halls to large audiences but he does give talks to groups in private houses. On several occasions, he has gone along in his ordinary clothes to give one of his talks, only to be greeted by expressions of disappointment because he has not turned up in his costume.

In November 2009, the Kesher group, a pro-Israel Christian organisation based in Peckham, invited Horan to perform his dance. Horan went along with a number of friends and was about to launch into an account of Israel's significance in the Bible when the group's organiser stopped Horan in his tracks, asking him to just do his peace dance.

His experience is that, 'It is often the very people to whom I am taking the message who ask the messenger to display himself'.

'Why should I refuse them, if that is what they want? Why should I refuse to do a good turn to people, if, for them, that is just what my costume and my dance do?'

Horan has had years of dealings with the medical profession but psychiatrists do not appear to agree on his mental state. Today, he continues to visit a psychiatrist once every three months.

He sees Dr Jed Boardman, a consultant working for the South London and Maudsley NHS Trust. He has got to know Dr Boardman well and chats to him with ease about life and religious beliefs. Dr Boardman continues to prescribe drugs, paroxetine and olanzapine, primarily to help Horan to cope with mild depression.

Church authorities remain officially silent on the troublesome cleric. As far as they are concerned, the entire saga was dealt with the day Cardinal Josef Ratzinger signed the decree that stripped Horan of his collar for good. Looking back, Horan holds no grudges against the Church or those at its helm. Quite the opposite. The Catholic Church, he says, gave him a sense of reverence. The exposition of the Blessed Sacrament conveyed a sense of the divine.

Horan's father's generation raised their caps when they passed a church, or when they heard the name of Jesus on the radio or television. There was the Mass and the ringing of bells at the Consecration, all of which created in Horan 'a feeling of respect, reverence and awe for heavenly things, for Almighty God and his son Jesus'. The Church also gave him an education from the age of five to twenty-six.

After all Horan's run-ins with the Church authorities, one man Bishop Charles Henderson, Auxiliary Bishop of Southwark for thirty-four years, still stands out in his mind. 'He was the best of the hierarchy to me. He met me the first day I arrived in Southwark diocese in August 1973. He met me in July 1994, at the very end of my time working in Southwark diocese. That covered a period of twenty-one years. He did his best for me, showing care, consideration and concern.'

However, Horan is critical of the how the Church failed to support him financially over the turbulent years. For about six years after he left his parish in 1994, Horan was sent Mass offerings. But since then, he claims they have given him nothing, despite the fact that the Church pays towards his accommodation on Howbury Road.

'They still don't (give money), but they do give it to Delia, as they have done for the past seven years. By right they should be giving it to me, but, by giving it to Delia, it is, in effect, like giving it to me, as without it, I would have to pay Delia far more rent. Father Hugh Bridge had to fight hard to get this concession from them. Without him, it is doubtful they would have given Delia a penny.'

In his home in Tralee, County Kerry, Dan Horan ponders his brother's life. Since childhood, he has remained very close to Neil, knowing him as an extremely kind and warm individual.

But Neil's ridiculous and sometimes downright dangerous and selfish actions over the years embarrassed and hurt his family. 'It has hurt,' Dan says, 'but I think it's all forgotten too and people have moved on from it. They still love Neil at the same time.'

More than anybody else, Dan Horan wants his brother to go on a 'talking tour'. A successful, self-made businessman, Dan Horan is willing to pay all the costs. 'I've told him, if he goes out there and explains his beliefs, he'll pack out the place. It's no good just having posters saying, "Read the Bible."'

'However, there's one condition: no more short kilt and jigs and acting the fool. It's time now for him to explain to the ordinary person what it is he actually believes.'

Neil Horan gives his brother's suggestion serious consideration: 'I will do it,' he says, 'when I think the time is right. I would love to stand before an audience and speak at length in a serious manner about the most serious matters on earth.'

It is fourteen years since Horan was home to his native County Kerry. For the first seven of these years, he claims there was no particular reason for not visiting, except that home in Scartaglen did not hold the same attraction for him since his parents, Nellie and Free, passed away, in January 1988 and February 1996 respectively. He believes feelings against him were strong in the aftermath of Silverstone and Athens. But six years on, he believes things have changed and predicts he will not be very much older before he travels home again.

If he were to travel to Ireland and accept his brother's idea of a lecture tour, Horan would be forced to confront a major credibility issue. In 1993, he publicly predicted that the second coming would occur by the year 2000. The millennium, Horan claimed, was so significant that it would likely herald the end of the world. In a booklet published by parishioners, entitled *Father Neil Horan: His Life and Work and His Present View of World Events*, he wrote: 'I am foretelling that the world, as we know it, will end and that Jesus will come before the year 2000. It may happen only days before, but I am predicting it will definitely happen by the last day of this century. If the first of January comes, the year 2000, and it has not happened, I will be proved wrong. I will say to everyone, from the bottom of my heart, forgive me for leading you astray.'

Horan did get it completely wrong. In March 2010, for the first time, the lifelong student of Bible prophecy publicly apologised: 'A full ten years have come and gone since that date, and the end of the world has still not come. I got it wrong, hopelessly wrong...

'I accept that I did predict a date, and for this I am truly sorry. The year 2000 was a mighty big date, the biggest since the time of Christ, but that does still not excuse the kind of over-zealous and definite forecast that I made. From the bottom of my heart, I ask you all to forgive me for leading you astray.' He went on to argue that although inspired, the prophets too got it wrong, as did generations of Christians over the past two thousand years. So too did the Seventh Day Adventists and the Jehovah's Witnesses. Like Horan, they are still waiting.

Among the few things in Horan's life that have remained consistent for more than thirty-five years is his stubborn belief that Christ will return to this earth and rule for 1000 years on the throne of David. It will come about as a conclusion to World War III; political establishments all over the world will be forced to surrender and become part of a commonwealth of Israel. The dead will be brought to life and those worthy will help to rule a new world government from Jerusalem. For Horan, it's not a question of if or when, but what happens thereafter.

In the meantime, he dances and waits.